Catharine Roseboom, Jacob Livingston Roseboom, Joseph Henry White, Henry Ulyate Swinnerton

1630-1897

A Brief History of the Ancestors and Descendants of John Roseboom (1739-1805)

and of Jesse Johnson (1745-1832)

Catharine Roseboom, Jacob Livingston Roseboom, Joseph Henry White, Henry Ulyate Swinnerton

1630-1897
A Brief History of the Ancestors and Descendants of John Roseboom (1739-1805) and of Jesse Johnson (1745-1832)

ISBN/EAN: 9783337417222

Printed in Europe, USA, Canada, Australia, Japan

Cover: Foto ©ninafisch / pixelio.de

More available books at **www.hansebooks.com**

1630-1897

A BRIEF HISTORY

OF THE

ANCESTORS AND DESCENDANTS

OF

JOHN ROSEBOOM
(1739-1805)

AND OF

JESSE JOHNSON
(1745-1832)

COMPILED BY

CATHARINE ROSEBOOM, Dr. J. LIVINGSTON ROSEBOOM,
Rev. HENRY U. SWINNERTON and JOSEPH H. WHITE.

CHERRY VALLEY, NEW YORK

Printed at The Co-operative Press, 114 Austin Street, Cambridge, Mass.

INTRODUCTION.

The twofold object in the preparation of this little work has been, first, to preserve to the descendants of HENDRICK JANSE ROSEBOOM, of Albany, N. Y., and Captain JOHN JOHNSON, of Roxbury, Mass., whatever information is obtainable regarding their early history in America; and, secondly, to afford as complete a record as possible of the families comprising the later generations, from about the time when the two lines were united by the marriage of Abraham Roseboom and Ruth Johnson, in Cherry Valley, N. Y., in 1806, yet not confining it strictly to their descendants. It contains no statements asserted as facts unless there is documentary or other sufficient evidence existing in proof thereof, and where the assertions made are matters of opinion, it is so stated.

It is not often easy to trace the history of early American families prior to their arrival in this country, for there is apt to be an abrupt break in crossing the ocean; and amidst the hardships attendant on those times the recording of events on this side was too often neglected or left to officials of church and town who took no interest in the performance of their duties other than in the easiest possible way. Hence the entries of church registers, town records and Bible data often vary. It would have been less difficult had the work been commenced a generation ago, since personal recollections might have yielded important items that are now unattainable. That which is known will, however, be of none the less interest to those who come after us.

If nothing were known of the origin of the Roseboom family the name itself would at once show that it was Holland Dutch, and of earlier Teutonic derivation. The first part has the same meaning in Dutch as in English, "Rose," and the second part signifies a tree, "Rose tree." The spelling is found under a number of variations in Holland, but in this country has been changed to its simplest form. Dr. J L. Roseboom, while traveling in Holland in 1885, found traces of the family not only in Amsterdam, but at the Hague, in Zwolle, and in other places in the northern provinces, but was unable to ascertain definite knowledge of Hendrick Janse Roseboom, or of his parents. Part of the early data has been taken from Munsell's "Collections on the History of Albany," Vol. IV; Talcott's "Genealogical Notes of New York and New England Families;" Pearson's "Albany County Records," Vols. I to IV; and other similar works. But these invaluable authorities are not invariably reliable, for instance, Jacob Roseboom, Jr., is credited with five sons named Johannes, the fourth of whom is recorded as " baptized Sept. 15, 1776, died at Cherry Valley, Mar. 15, 1829." This Johannes, or John, belonged in a different branch of the family. It was John, the son of Lieut. John Roseboom and Susannah Veeder, born Oct. 25, 1774, who died in Cherry Valley on the date mentioned.

We have been unable to ascertain the relationship of this Jacob, Jr., to Hendrick Janse, as the latter had only one grandson named Jacob, and there is no record of his having a son Jacob. Jacob, Jr., married, Jan. 20, 1763, Hester Lansing, a direct descendant of Gerrit Frederick Lansing, the father of the wife of Hendrick Janse, and left a large number of descendants. Jacob, son of Hendrick Roseboom and Debora Staats, was doubtless the man who was associated with John Lindesay and others in the Cherry Valley patent; he was baptized July 14, 1695, and at the time the patent was granted (1739) would have been about 44 years old; he is the only one of the name appearing on the records whose age would warrant this assumption. Munsell does not mention Elizabeth, dau. of Hendrick Janse Roseboom, nor does he mention Hendrick, oldest son of Gerrit Roseboom and Maria Sanders; and there may be other errors; the above facts have been obtained from other sources. Owing to the same christian names occurring so frequently in all the families it is very difficult to determine just where each individual belonged, and we may have made mistakes or perpetuated the errors of the historians to whom we are indebted for so much of what we present to our readers.

Of the early Johnsons, information has been derived from Drake's "History of Roxbury, Mass.," Savage's "Genealogical Dictionary," and other authorities on New England history.

We give as complete a history as possible of the ancestors, in the male line, of Lieut. John Roseboom, (1735-1805), and of Jesse Johnson, (1745-1832), and then include a record of their descendants, separating the latter into respective lines of descent, beginning with the eldest married child of Lieut. Roseboom. Each family has a distinctive number, and the number in parenthesis following the names of the parents refers to the family number of such parents, while the number at the right of the records of the children refers to their individual records which follow. Where no such figures are given the children were not married. A few sketches of the lives of those unmarried have been interspersed among the others. An appendix has been added, containing papers relating to the Roseboom family, and letters of reference to those papers are placed in the book. Only such abbreviations have been used as will be readily understood without explanation. The foot-notes, we feel sure, will be appreciated by many who, while not in direct line, have been connected with the families by collateral marriages.

INTRODUCTION.

Previous to 1753 the year, in England and her colonies, commenced on the 25th day of March, while the New Style had been adopted by other countries in 1582. Hence arose the custom of using a double date for that part of the year between Jan. 1 and Mar. 25, as 1743-4, or 1743/4. We have deemed it best to use the New Style date in such cases.

There is a tradition that the coat of arms of the Roseboom family was "a ship." Nothing definite has been discovered as to this, but the following arms assumptive have been used: —

Azure, a cross argent, charged with a rose gules and three churches proper. *Crest*, a red rose expanded. *Motto*, *Pro Deo et ecclesiam*.

The family badge is a sprig of wild rose.

We sincerely thank all who have so kindly given their assistance in our work, and if the possessors of this volume will faithfully use the margins and blank pages to perpetuate the records in the years to come, our labors will be amply rewarded.

CATHARINE ROSEBOOM,
DR. J. L. ROSEBOOM,
REV. H. U. SWINNERTON,
JOSEPH HENRY WHITE.

INDEX TO FAMILIES.

The numbers after the names refer to the Families in which each is to be found.

Allen, Elizabeth G.,	27	French, William C.,	93
" Helen M.,	21	Gansevoort, Conrad,	23
Angel, Catherine E.,	22	" Elizabeth,	11
Aspinwall, Eliza,	61	" James,	19
Bartholomew, Florence,	101	" John R.,	13
Belcher, Abraham R.,	41	" Dr. Ten Eyck,	14
" Susan M.,	34	Gill, Maria S.,	113
Bon Durant, Lucy E.,	70	Goodwin, Lucy,	77
Brand, Harriet A.,	64	" Lucy W.,	86
Brockett, Lucy M.,	52	Griswold, Hattie M.,	103
Carroll, Mary,	57	Hall Elizabeth,	39
Churchill, Elizabeth,	71	" James S.,	46
Cooke, Catharine E.,	16	" William E.,	48
" Dr. Henry G.,	25	Hazard, Catharine E.,	16
" Robert W.,	26	Hess, Mary L.,	20
" Susan,	15	Hessert, Grace H.,	114
Cortelyou, Eunice M.,	47	Hoagland, Phebe E.,	91
Damon, George T.,	58	Howell, Mary L.,	20
" Sarah M.,	54	Huggins, Caroline I.,	56
Dunlap, Mary S.,	116	Hungerford, Mary W.,	24
Edwards, Arabella S.,	29	Inglehart, Fred M.,	112
" Helen G.,	30	" George N.,	111
Ely, Sarah,	40	" Sarah M.,	109
Farquharson, Mary A.,	99	" Sarah W.,	117
Ford, Jessie B.,	104	Johnson, Daniel,	8
French, Deloss D.,	94	" Daniel, Jr.,	9
" Horace W.,	95	" Erastus,	115
" Leroy E.,	92	" Capt. Isaac,	6
" Mary L.,	80	" Isaac, Jr.,	7
" Susan,	83	" Jesse,	10

INDEX TO FAMILIES.

Johnson, Capt. John,	5	
" Robert,	50	
" Sally M.,	106	
" William H.,	108	
" William S.,	110	
Judd, Cynthia E.,	118	
" Hubert,	119	
Keeney, Clara M.,	55	
Kennedy, Lucy,	105	
Long, Henrietta,	72	
Lord, Mary E.,	107	
Mackay, Helen G.,	31	
McCollum, Marietta,	67	
Magee, Catharine E.,	22	
Merritt, Lucy J.,	65	
Newcomb, Susan R.,	88	
Ogden, Elizabeth,	18	
Pardee, Mary E.,	120	
Presley, Ella C.,	98	
Ransbothan, Mary L.,	89	
Rice, Annetta S.,	96	
Ringland, Jane S.	87	
Roseboom, Abraham,	33	
" Abraham H.,	43	
" Barent,	32	
" Hendrick J.,	1	
" Hendrick M.,	3	
" Henry,	35	
" Jesse J.,	37	
" Lieut. John,	4	
" Myndert,	2	
Sawyer, Ruth,	44	
Schenck, Sarah E.,	45	
Shannon, Lucy,	38
Stewart, Daniel,	60
" Elizabeth,	59
" George P.,	69
" Henry R.,	63
" John R.,	66
" Robert S.,	68
" Samuel, Jr.,	62
Stockton, Annetta S.,	96
Strong, Lucy L.,	102
Swinnerton, Levantia L.,	42
Taylor, La Royal,	84
" Lester D.,	85
" Mary L.,	75
" Royal C.,	97
" Wilder B.,	100
Thacher, Maria M.,	51
" Robert J.,	53
Underhill, Minerva E.,	28
Van Vranken, Gansevoort,	17
" Maria,	12
White, Marietta,	36
Wilder, Austin J.	81
" Calvin,	74
" Deloss D.,	82
" Eli T.,	78
" Horace,	76
" Mary,	73
" Orville H.,	90
" Seth L.,	79
Wilson, Eliza,	61
Yates, Mary L.,	49

PERSONS CONNECTED WITH THE FAMILIES BY MARRIAGE.

The numbers after the names refers to the Families in which each is to be found.

———, Margery,	5
Allen, Gerrard,	27
" William W.,	21
Angel, Benjamin F.,	22
Arnold, Edith,	9
Aspinwall, Dr. Eleazar,	61
Ballou, Mary D.,	43
Bartholomew, George A.,	101
Belcher, Moses,	34
BouDurant, William,	70
Brainard, Carmelia,	85
Brand, Nelson S.,	64
Brinckerhoff, Mary C.,	17
Brockett, Dr. Linus P.,	52
Carroll, Frank H.,	57
Churchill, Frank A.,	71
Clark, Mary A.,	119
Cleveland, Anna B.,	84
Coleman, Phebe J.,	76
Cook, Caroline,	37
Cooke, Ambrose W.,	16
" Dr. Robert W.,	15
Cortelyou, Gansevoort V. V.,	47
Cowdrey, Maria B.,	25
Cuthbertson, Margaret,	111
Damon, Orlo R.,	54
Dunlap, James B.,	116
Edwards, Alfred L.,	29
Edwards, Lewis,	30
Ely, Richard,	40
Ensign, Eliza,	60
Farquharson, Van Densen,	99
Fawer, Grace,	5
Fenn, Cornelia M.,	23
Finch, Maranda F.,	82
Ford, Burton J.,	104
French, Watson E.,	80, 83
Gansevoort, Conrad,	11
Gill, James B.,	113
Goodwin, Abigail,	10
" Clinton,	86
" Dr. Erastus,	77
Griswold, William H.,	103
Grout, Lydia B.,	79
Hall, William,	39
Harris, Mary,	7
Hazard, John V S.,	16
Hess, Hiram R.,	20
Hessert, George,	114
Hoagland, Frank,	91
Holt, Jerusha W.,	115
Howell, Edward, Jr.,	20
Huggins, Ploudon R.,	56
Hungerford, John N.,	24
Inglehart, Dr. Smith,	109, 117
Irwin, Rebecca,	13

PERSONS CONNECTED WITH THE FAMILIES.

Jacobsen, Tryntje J.,	1
Johnson, Dr. Ebenezer,	106
Judd, John,	118
Keeney, Albert B.,	55
Kendig, Larissa M.,	78
Kennedy, Dr. James,	105
Kerwood, Mary J.,	92
Kitchen, Della,	48
Lansing, Gysbertje,	1
Leek, Abigail,	8
Le Sueur, Cora E.,	46
Livingston, Cornelia R.,	35
Long, John H.,	72
Lord, Rev. John C.,	107
Lyon, Helen R.,	14
Mackay, Archibald K.,	31
McCollum, DeWitt C.,	67
McLean, Elizabeth J.,	41
Magee, Duncan S.,	22
Mead, Nellie,	58
Merrill, Carrie F.,	90
Merritt, Dr. George,	65
Mossholder, Eliza E.,	68
Moxley, Fannie E.,	95
Newcomb, Ozro R.,	88
Norton, Phebe,	62
Ogden, Eliza,	19
" Henry A.,	18
Pardee, Dr. Howard A.,	120
Pickett, Marinda,	81
Pike, Sylvia J.,	97
Porter, Elizabeth,	6
Presley, Fred E.,	98
Ransbothan, George H.,	89
Rayder, Celeste,	69
Rhinehart, Maria E.,	63
Rice, Herbert A.,	96
Richards, Kate F.,	110
Richardson, Jane,	9
" Marilla A.,	93
Richardson, Mary E.,	94
Ringland, William D.,	87
Rowley, Marietta E.,	100
Sawyer, John,	44
Schenck, Dr. Peter L.,	45
Schermerhorn, Sarah,	32
Shannon, James,	38
Sheldon, Mary M.,	66
Smith, Carrie L.,	93
" Ellen P.,	66
Southwick, Martha S.,	53
Stevens, Lizzie,	112
Stevenson, Mary,	10
Stewart, Samuel,	59
Stockton, Thomas V.,	96
Strong, Emmet J.,	102
Swinnerton, Rev. Henry U.,	42
Taylor, Lester,	75
Ten Eyck, Maria,	3
Thacher, Rev. Washington,	51
Thayer, Harriet,	79
Thomas, Mary H.,	81
Tryon, Sarah,	9
Tyms, Catharine,	32
Underhill, Edwin S.,	28
Van Mater, Hulda H.,	6
Van Vranken, Rev. Samuel A.,	12
Veeder, Susanna,	4
Vinhagen, Maria,	2
Wakefield, Julia W.,	78
Ward, Elizabeth,	9
Wheeler, Mary A.,	108
White, Dr. Joseph,	36
Wilcox, Lucy,	50
Wilder, Col. Eli,	73
" Phebe,	74
Wilson, Josephine,	46
" William M.,	61
Yates, Dr. Nathaniel F.,	49

THE ROSEBOOMS.

1. The first ancestor of the family of Roseboom in this country was "HENDERICK ROOSENBOOM," as it appears in the inaccurate spelling of the earliest document where it is found, or "Henderyck Yannsen Rooseboom," as it stands, "with his own hand set," at the foot of the same writing. He appears to have come from Holland about the year 1655. Although this date, as well as the dates of his birth and marriage, is wanting, the extant records concerning him are remarkably full and circumstantial. He died in 1703, "an old man;" he could scarcely have been less than thirty years of age when he first becomes known to us as an active man upon the scene of affairs, in positions of trust, and possessed of substantial means, in 1662. He may have been born about 1630, and not improbably earlier.

The particular locality in the Netherlands from which he came is also unknown, but several indications point to the district East of the Zuider Zee. The Lansings, his wife's people, came from Hasselt, in Overyssell. Rooseboooms now living at the Hague came from Dalen, in Drenthe, and the ancestors of others living at Arnhem* came from Elburg, in the same province of Gelderland. Finally, a letter of inquiry concerning family relationships was sent many years since to Abraham Roseboom, of Cherry Valley, by one of the name at Harderwyk, Gelderland. These places are but a few miles apart,

---

* Gerrit Hendrick Rooseboom was a "Burgemeester" of Elburg, Gelderland; whose son, Hendrick Ernsts Rooseboom, was "Ontvanger" (treasurer), and (born about 1769) died there in 1853. Reije Rut (Rutgers) Geeris Jans Rooseboom, his son, was living at Arnhem in 1885. Willem Rooseboom, his son, resides at Baakerstraat, 52, that city. A number of the art treasures of Amsterdam and the Hague are by an admired lady artist, Margaret Rooseboom.

and from some one of them in all probability the pioneer set out for the wilds of the "Nieuwe Niederlanden." Whether his marriage took place in Holland or after he reached the new world; whether any of his children were born in the old home, is uncertain. The Albany church records "are wanting, previous to 1684, from that date they are complete," so that we are deprived of any data which might have been derived from the records of the baptism of his children. But it seems most probable that, having emigrated with the family of his future wife, the Lansings, he married in Albany some years subsequent to his arrival, and that the date of that event was about 1660; for the eldest son, Johannes, went among the Indians in 1685, "to the Ottawas, back of Virginia," and was married Nov. 18, 1688. He may be supposed to have been about twenty-five at the time.

The patronymic middle-name, Yannsen, Jannsen, or Janse, indicates that Hendrick's father's name was Jan, or Johannes, i. e., John; which is further supported by the circumstances that the eldest son,—who from an almost invariable custom bore the name of the grandparent,—was also so named: and this is all that is known of his ancestry.

The earliest mention of the family name is in the name of a ship so called, in a letter sent from Foort Nieuw Amstel, i. e., New Castle, Delaware, by J. Aldrich, dated Nov. 14, 1657, "To the Noble, Honorable, Worshipful, Wise, Very Prudent Mr. Petrus Stuyvesant, Director General of New Netherlands Residing at the Mahattans in Fort Amsterdam, by the Roseboom, which God may guide." This is found in Vol. XII of the Colonial Documents, p. 202. And on p. 203. "The above is a copy of my last by the Roseboom, Reynier de Vries, Skipper, (shipmaster)." Other references to this ship occur in the Holland Documents, pp. 456, 466, as follows: "Laus Deo A° 1663. Amsterdam in New Netherland. (Powder account.) To extraordinary acct. of the Hon. Majores for following, ... also received with ship Rooseboom, Pieter Ryersen Van der Beer, skipper, 6 kegs containing 600 lbs. powder A 35 gl.*

---

* The money of accounts of the Dutch was the gilder or florin and stuiver, 20 of the latter to one of the former. There were the guilder sewant and the guilder beaver; the latter of the value of about 40 cents, or three times that of the former. The guilder of accounts was commonly valued at one shilling, New York currency. The term pounds among the Dutch must not be considered as pounds sterling; they were 20 New York shillings, and equalled $2.50.

per 100 weight with st. 5. 8 charges, according to invoice of the 24 March, 1663, 600 lbs." "Port duty, received for right of anchorage from the following ships — the Rooseboom, Pieter Ryenson, skipper, 100." (Gunner's delivery book.) " 1664. August 17, to 16 lbs. fired when the ship Roseboom sailed for Patria." Whether this vessel was named for or owned by the subject of this sketch, or whether it was merely a sentimental name, " Rosetree," like " Mayflower," "Half moon," etc., will probably never be known; but it is while she is making her voyages that de Heer Henderyck Jannse appears among the dwellers on the upper Hudson.

Preserved among the Fort Orange Records of date 1660. May 27, is the "petition of Jan Dircksen van Bremen, Albert James von Volckenburgh, et al., praying that Dutch as well as Indians brokers be employed to trade with the Indians," and among the names appended is " Henderick Roseboom." The other party were for prohibiting all Europeans, " Christians," from treading the forest paths, thus excluding civilization. The first date after this is Sept. 13, 1662, when he purchased a house and lot " in the village of Beverwyck, on the hill," and from this time on his name is found in numerous authentic documents in the annals of Albany. The property mentioned was of historical interest, having been patented to Pieter Bronck. " As it stands with all that is fast by earth and nailed, and as great as the patent thereof mentions," it was conveyed by Reyndert Pieterse (Bronck?) and Jacob Herick (Gerick), " for the sum of 550 guilders, payable in good merchantable beavers, at eight guilders apiece, in two installments, in July '63 and '64," the two " sellers" setting their " marks," but Rooseboom writing his name with his own hand. November 16, of that year, he is surety with J. J. Schermerhooren for Jurriaen Janssen in the purchase of a house from the estate of Andries Herbertsen, for the benefit of the widow.

The exact situations of the ancient properties in Albany have been carefully ascertained and mapped, so that we can fix the precise spot where this ancestor lived. It lay on the east side of North Pearl street, northward of Maiden Lane. The palisades constituting the northerly fortifications of the settlement passed through the middle of the land-plat, and the name of " Roseboom's gate" was given to the exit which existed at that point, the " Burghers' blockhouse" being adjacent. Mynheer Rooseboom was a "trader" by occupation, and as the Indians gathered particularly at this gate for barter, the spot was regarded as the most advantageous one for business purposes. In subsequent years as the place grew we find repeated descriptions of land conveyed "upon the hill without the gate by Rooseboom's."

Less than a month later, October 5th, of the same year, he appears before the clerk and commissaries of Fort Orange and Beverwyck with his sureties to take over from Jan Gerritse Van Marcken the office of " Farmer (Pacht) of the Slaughter Excise," for the collection of revenue from the butchering of beasts of all kinds throughout the settlement, the office having been offered to the highest bidder, and his bid being 750 guilden. Every animal slaughtered was taxed one stuiver for each guilden of its worth, or if paid for in beaver-skins, (a very usual currency) 20 stuivers per beaver "in good seewant," i. e., wampum, (seawant). Mr. Roseboom held this office in subsequent years, paying 790 guilders at one time, and making his payments to the authorities quarterly. A similar "Wine and Beer Excise" was bid off at 2900 g. by other parties, but it was carefully specified in this case that the seewant be " well strung, 12 white and 8 black to the stuiver." Perhaps the topers got tangled up and broke the strings of their wampum, and at times could not tell white from black !

The sobriety of character implied by this distinction suits well with Hendrick Rooseboom's appointment to the office of Voorlezer, or Public Reader, in the ancient Reformed Protestant church, a position which confirms the impression that he was a man of education and of character commanding respect. The first mention of this is some years after his appointment, in a petition of the Lutherans of Willemstadt, dated 1674, for leave to bury their dead, remonstrating against employing the official of the Reformed church. It runs : " To the Rt. Honble Myn Heer Anthony Colve, Governr General of N. Netherland — Those of the Ausburgh confession represent with due respect, that your Petitioners are ordered in cases of burial of their dead to pay the Sexton (Aansprecker) of the Reformed Church, notwithstanding they employ their own Sexton. It is also wel known to all that Mr. Roosenboom hath addressed a petition on that subject to the Honble Heer General above named, to be favored therein ; which petition had no result, but the Heer Laval being come up, said in full court, in date the 7th Nov., 1672, he had authority as to Roosenboom's petition." Wherefore they argue. " Let the Dead bury their Dead; for with what free conscience can your Precentor go and act for the Lutherans, for they have more ceremonies than the Reformed? Whereupon at that time he had no more to say, and it was as well. Wherefore your Petitioners, for aforesaid reasons, approach your Honour requesting most humbly that they may enjoy what they have been granted; and as Your Petitioners, Brethren at N. Orange, enjoy the same, that they further may bury their dead without notifying Mr. Roosenboom, but employ their own Sexton and no one else. Whereupon they expect a favorable answer. Your Honors affectionate Subjects, Bernhardus Anthony, V. D. M."

The terms " sexton " and " precentor " here occurring are the English translations of the two Dutch words expressive of functions discharged by the Voorlezer in connection with his proper capacity as church reader, as is seen from later documents, although the titles are used indifferently and are much confused in the translations, owing to the difference of the customs prevailing among the English. Thus, " Mayor's court Nov. 19, 1695, Whereas Hend Roseboom, Voorlezer in ye church of ye Citty of Albany doth appear here & desyreth that consideration may be used that his sallery may be paid, being he stand in need of ye same." Again, in 1701, " Ye Petition of Hend. Roseboom ye Church Reader," is laid before the Supervisors by " ye Justices of ye Citty & County," and payment advised. The Voorlezer seems to have suffered as much from dilatory payments as some servants of the church in later times. Funerals were affairs of the utmost pomp, and expense which the estates of the deceased could bear, the estimation in which they were held being gauged by the splendor of the occasion. The Aansprecker, literally " inviter," the person sent round with invitations to a funeral, conducted the ceremonies as undertaker, a function which went with that of Leader of the responses in public worship, including the reading of sermons in the absence of a clergyman. On the other hand, the labor of grave digging was discharged by another person, as will appear further on. The Voorlezer would usually be the Voorzinger, or precentor, as well, and the former office seems gradually to have been replaced by the latter.* This office Mr. Roseboom held till his death in 1703.

In the course of years changes have taken place. The English have become masters of the colony, in 1664; the two hamlets of Beverwyck and Fort Orange have coalesced into "ye Citty of Albany," chartered in 1686, and de Heer Roseboom's name, under the influence of the English spelling, has lost one element of its first long vowel, being now spelled Roseboom. He himself has grown to be the "Senior" of a band who bear the family name, his four sons being now in or towards middle life and sharing the responsibilities and honors of the community and the church, while his two daughters are married and have families. Careful search of the records, where his and his sons' names appear frequently almost every year for years together, fails to discover mention of any other individual of the name, and the conclusion is sufficiently certain that all the Albany Roseboombs are descended from him.†

The Stuart dynasty had been replaced by the Dutch William of Orange in 1688. The good Mary had died; a growing disfavor against the foreigners had vented itself in the Commons by acts of jealousy towards the great stadtholder king, culminating in 1698 with the dismissal of his trusty Dutch guards, "gentlemen who had lost

---

* "In July 1802, Mr. William Groesbeeck, who had been clerk of the church for a great number of years, died, and the desk he had occupied was hung in mourning. He was succeeded by his sons, Cornelius and David, who were the last of the Voorzingers."—*Annals of Albany*, Vol. 1, p. 120.

† Many distinct lines point to this conclusion. Although Hendrick's name appears in 1660, '62, '63, '64, '65, '66, '73, '74, '77, a period of 17 years, yet the name of no other Roseboom can be found during that time. Secondly, the very earliest mention of others beside himself is when, in 1683, Dominie Dellius, at the end of the year, made remembrance of the church members. His list includes eight Roseboombs, as follows: Hendrick, who is number 36, and Gysbertje Roseboom [dau. of Lansing], his wife, 37. Then comes Johannes, 130; Margaret 131; Maria Sanders [now Roseboom], 390; Gerritje Coslers [now Roseboom], 391; Hendrick, Jr., 420; Lysbeth, 465. These are all identified as members of the one family, and their wives. Tryntje Rutger is number 90, and after her name is written "now Rosebom," evidently inserted when she, later married Hendrick. Thirdly, a list of Heads of Families in Albany, June 1697, gives the following, who are none other than the same family, and mentions none besides.

Names.		Men.	Women.	Children.
Hendrick Roseboom		1	1	1
Johannes	"	1	1	3
Hendrick	"	1	1	2
Gerrit	"	1	1	3
Myndert	"	1	0	0

Again, a collection of the dates of the baptism of Hendrick's grandchildren, with the names of their sponsors, established the same, the rigidity of the old Dutch customs in such matters lending serviceable aid to the inquiry.

everything but their swords" for England's good. Perhaps this feeling of antipathy to Netherlanders accounts for the requirement of an "Oath of Allegiance to the King" from the residents of Albany, Jan. 4, 1699. Among the subscribers to this oath are the five names of Henderick Roseboom and his sons, Johannes, Gerrit, Henderick and Myndert. Again no others of the name appear.

A glimpse of household life is afforded by a Public Sale, in the clerkship of Joh. Provoost, of the possessions of one Janse Kroon, giving the names of the purchasers and the articles and prices paid, in florins (guilders). While Philip Pieterse Schuyler (the first Mayor) carries off a "great tin pail," Henderick, our ancestor, gets a "copper stewpan," for which he pays f. 15.15; f. 3.00 for an "iron chaffing dish;" f. 4.05 for "an iron pot hanger;" and f. 2.00 for "a *bort* (board?) almanac," (i. e., to hang on the wall), besides some "little earthern platters" and "*hele* (?) and an old pillow bier" (perhaps a kind of lounge?). A touch of love for art and decoration is seen in the purchase of "pictures" in two lots of three each, besides "two little pictures," at f. 2.00, 1.15, and 5.00. What would not his descendants give to know what these pictures were?

The end of all things earthly came to the old man at last. On Sept. 15, 1702, he as "Sexton of this Citty appear in Common Council and desyres they will be pleased to confirm him in said office." This was granted, but the next mention of him is after his death, which occurred Nov. 4, 1703. His successor is after his office and its avails: "Dec. 13, 1703. Anthony Bratt, by his petition of ye Commonality, humbly prays, since Mr. Hendrik Roseboom, late Sexton of this Citty, deceased, that they will be pleased to appoint him to attend and doe ye services of ye said office of Sexton in such Manner as ye same lately did appertain unto ye said Roseboom and to grant him ye like Perquisites thereof. The Commonality, takeing ye said Petition into consideration, have granted ye said office of Sexton of ye Citty together with ye Perquisites thereof unto ye said Bratt, in such Manner as ye same was given and granted unto ye said Roseboom always provided that John Ratcliffe shall yet continue in ye service of that office and receive such perquisites thereof for digging of graves as he did in ye time and being of ye sd Mr. Roseboom, deceased."

He married. 1st, probably in Albany, about 1660. GYSBERTJE

LANSING, dau. of Gerrit Frederick Lansing. She was born in the town of Hasselt, in the Province of Overyssell, Holland.

He married, 2nd, Dec. 5, 1695, TRYNTJE JANSE JACOBSEN,* dau. of Johannes Van Breestede, and widow of Rutger Jacobsen. This marriage is thus recorded in the church records: "Hendrick Roseboom, de oude weduwenaar van Gysbertje Lansing, en Tryntje Janse, weduwe van Rut Jacobse." Which is to say, "Henderick Roseboom, the aged widower of Gysbertje Lansing and Tryntje Janse, widow of Rutger Jacobsen." In the enlightened municipal system which prevailed among the Netherlanders the birth of infants was supervised by persons properly authorized, and Vrouw Jacobsen held this trust in the days of her widowhood by license from the authorities. In 1701 this good wife is recorded as "on a jury," upon what inquest is not said; it may have been as a witness. She died in 1711.

It is difficult to place the children of Hendrick Janse Roseboom in the order of their birth owing to the meager records of those early days. From the most reliable sources at command we conclude that Johannes was the eldest, but as Elizabeth is not mentioned except in the list of early church members, we are in doubt where to place her in the list of children, but there is little doubt that Myndert was the youngest. It is probable that they were born in nearly the following order. A more complete record of their marriages and their children will be found in the appendix.

CHILDREN:— by the first marriage.

1. *Johannes,* m. Nov. 18, 1688, Gerritje Coster. (a)
2. *Margarita,* m. Nov. 15, 1685, Pieter Thomase Mingael. (b)
3. *Gerrit,* m. Nov. 24, 1689, Maria Sanders. (c h)
4. *Hendrick,* m. Nov. 1, 1694, Debora Staats. (d)
5. *Elizabeth,* m. Jan. 13, 1692, Willem Jacobse Van Deusen. (e)
6. *Myndert,* m. Maria Vinhagen. (2)

---

* Tryntje Janse Van Breestede married, 1st, June 3, 1646, Rutger Jacobsen Van Schoenderwoert, otherwise known as Rutger Jacobsen and Rut Van Woert, who died in 1665.

CHILDREN.

1. *Margaret,* b. 1647; m. Jan. 2, 1667, Jan Janse Bleecker; d. 1733.
2. *Engeltje,* bap. Apr. 10, 1650; m. Melgert Abrahamse Van Duesen; bur. July 11, 1728.
3. *Harmen.*

This Harmen was probably born in Beverwyck soon after his father moved there. He had two sons Anthony and Harmen who settled in New York, one of whom was probably the ancestor of Cornelia Rutgers Livingston who married Henry Roseboom.

Capt. Johannes Roseboom, son of Hendrick J. Roseboom and Gysbertje Lansing, (1), was probably born in Albany, about 1661. His parents had two daughters and four sons, of whom the youngest, Myndert, is the ancestor of those descendants to whom this account particularly relates. The dates of their birth and baptism being lost, we are left to infer from Dominie Dellius's list of church members, that if they were received as communicants in the order of their seniority, Johannes would be the eldest child, and the others succeed thus:—Margaretta, Hendrick, Elizabeth, Gerrit, Myndert. The two youngest, however, were received at dates subsequent to that list, as was also Deborah Staats, who became the wife of the younger Hendrick. Their marriages, all but Myndert's, are recorded, following a different order, naturally; and the births or baptisms of most of their children, together with the sponsors, who were all but invariably near relatives, are also on record. (f) From these data a somewhat complete statistical history can be made out, and abundant references exist to show the civil standing and social position of the family.

Capt. Johannes was a "trader," and previous to his marriage his life was adventurous. In the Colonial History, Vol. V, p. 76, we read of a distant expedition of which he was the head, "In or about the year 1685 Col. Dongan, the governor of New York, sent one Roseboom, an inhabitant of Albany, with ten or twelve men, to invite the Ottawawas (a people on the back of Maryland, Virginia and Carolina) to come and trade at Albany." This general statement is more fully explained in Vol. III, where we find that "Capt. Roseboom," on a second trip, which was evidently in the direction of what we now call Canada, made a number of these Indians prisoners, and that in restoring them the next year to their tribe by Dongan's orders, was himself captured by a French expedition. On p. 422 there is first a brief reference to the capture of the Indians: —"August, 1687, Ottawa Indian prisoners sent home by Capt. Roseboom last Fall." Then follows, p. 476, a letter from Gov. Dongan to a Capt. Palmer, in which the affair is described thus: "The King's subjects here, living plentifully, have not regarded the making discoveries into the country until late, being discouraged by me. One Roseboom had leave in the year 1685 to go with some young men as far as the Ottawawas and Twiswicks, where they were well received and wanted to come every year. . . . But a little after their being out, attacked a castle of their's and took five or six hundred prisoners, and brought them away to their own country; which, when I heard of, I ordered delivered to Roseboom and to one Major McGregory, a Scot gentleman, who went with sixty of the young men of Albany and some Albany Indians, (a beaver-trading to those further nations) as many of those prisoners as were willing to return home. The Governor of Canada hearing of their going that way, sent 200 French and 300 or 400 Indians to intercept them, and has taken them prisoners, taken their goods from them, and what further danger is not known." There are other references to the capture of Roseboom and McGregory by the French, and serious troubles grew out of Governor De Norville's sentencing to death one of Roseboom's troop. The French invaded the territory of the Iroquois in 1684 and '87, but were repelled with loss, jealousy of the Indian trade and barter being the constant source of irritation.

The family of the old Voorlezer were prominent among the upholders of the church, his sons and sons-in-law sustaining office repeatedly. Ever since the English had had possession of the country the ancient Reformed Protestant body had existed by sufferance, without recognition as a "church." In petition to the King, George I, Aug. 10, 1720, by the church it is "set forth, that the inhabitants of Albany, descended of Dutch ancestors have from the first settlement of this province by Christians, hitherto held, used and enjoyed the free and undisturbed exercise of their religion and worship in the Dutch language, after the manner of the Reformed Protestant religion in Holland, according to the common rules, institutions and church government of the national Synod of Dort, in Holland, A. D., 1616." In answer to which an Act of Incorporation is granted, and Johannes Roseboom and William Jacobse Van Deusen (husband of Elizabeth Roseboom) are named as two among the four elders; and Myndert Roseboom, one among the four deacons, who with the minister were to make up the consistory "at the time of this our grant." Truly, they "seemed to be pillars."

In 1692 Johannes was an assistant alderman, and in 1700 alderman of the 2nd Ward, holding office several times. In 1700 he is serving at Fort Albany as Lieut. in Capt. Johannes Bleecker's company, and in 1715 "John Roseboom" (possibly his son) is Captain of a company of foot, in which "Hendrick Roseboom," who may be brother, son or nephew, is later appointed Lieutenant.

Capt. Johannes Roseboom was listed as "head of a family" with three children June, 1697; took the Oath of Allegiance next after his father, 1699, and by 1706 has four more children. For the record of his family see appendix, a. He "was buried in the church," Jan. 25, 1745, aged about 84.

2. MYNDERT ROSEBOOM, the second in this line of ancestral names, was the youngest son of Hendrick Janse Roseboom and Gysbertje Lansing, (1), and was born in Albany. His wife's name is given as Maria Vinhagen. He is the only one of this line about whose identity a degree of uncertainty seemed to hang, till dispelled by close investigation. This was owing to the unusual lack of recorded church data for his birth or baptism and his marriage, to confusion as to his wife's identity, and to the fact that the oldest Family Record says nothing of his ancestory and does not give his wife's name, while recording both his and her death. It is therefore necessary to present the evidence by which the often-mentioned Myndert Roseboom, deacon, is identified with the Myndert to whom the ancestry traces in Hendrick (Myndertse) Roseboom's Dutch Bible.

A copy of this valued Family Record is preserved in the English Bible of John J. Roseboom. It is drawn up from the point of view of Myndert's son Hendrick, and in very brief terms, giving first the births of Hendrick and his brethren, then their and the parents' deaths, then the marriage and children of Hendrick. With the latter we are not now concerned. The always popular name of Maria (Mary) occasions pitfalls, as there are Marias before and after, and on both sides, and it is to be recognized in Maritje, also.

The Record referred to is as follows:—

BIRTHS.

1707, Sep. 15, was born Hendrick Roseboom, in Albany.
1709, Sep. 23, was born Maria Roseboom,   "   "
1711, Sep. 2, was born Margaret Roseboom, "   "
1713, Sep. 1, was born Alida Roseboom,   "   "
1716, Jan. 11, was born John Roseboom,   "   "

DEATHS.

1722, Oct. 20, Myndert Roseboom, their father, died.
1722, Dec. 16, Maria Roseboom died.
1741, Apr. 6, Margaret Roseboom died.
1760, Feb. 28, their mother, the Widow of Myndert Roseboom, died.
1770, July 20, Alida Van Schaick died.
1783, Apr. 11, John Roseboom died.

We have here, first, the Bible record of Myndert Roseboom's death, Oct. 20, 1722; in the Dutch church records of Burials (g) is found, "1722, Oct. 22, Myndert Roseboom was buried." This is evidently the same man, the interment coming two days later than the death. He had been received into the church as a communicant, Apr. 9, 1676, four years later than his brother Gerrit, and the last one of his generation. He was the youngest of the family, perhaps by several years, yet he was old enough to take the Oath of Allegiance in 1699. If required to be 21 to do this his birth would be not later than 1678. He was sponsor at two baptisms in 1706, appearing in that capacity in his appropriate place as the last of the brothers. He held some unimportant offices; in 1702–3–5 he was constable of the second ward, high constable and juryman; a freeholder in 1720, and was one of the deacons named in the Act of Incorporation of the church that year, and was again mentioned as deacon the next year.

Marrying about 1706, the year when he was twice recorded as sponsor, his first child being recorded as baptised in 1707, why was not his marriage recorded, and who was his wife? The marriage may have taken place in some other town, of course. The printed authorities state that his wife was MARIA VINHAGEN, but where this information is obtained does not appear; yet his wife's name was Maria, as follows from the evidence, for while the Bible record states, "1760, Feb. 28, their mother, the Widow of Myndert Roseboom, died," not vouchsafing her name, and the church record does not give her burial, yet the two daughters, Maria and Margaret, who died before her, are recorded in the church burials at corresponding dates as children of Maria Roseboom, the one record supplementing the other, thus:

FAMILY RECORD.	CHURCH BURIALS.
1722, Dec. 16, Maria Roseboom died.	1722, Dec. 18, Maria Roseboom's child.
1741, Apr. 6, Margaret Roseboom died.	1741, Apr. 9, Margaretje, dau. of Maria Roseboom.

~Thus the widow Maria was called to bury her husband in October, and her daughter Maria at the age of 13, in December of the same year. Nineteen years later the second daughter followed, at the age of 29, but she is said by the authorities to have married Robert Lansing, although no intimation of this is given in the Bible record. The third daughter, Alida, who married Van Schaick, who was afterwards Mayor in 1756–'61, is recorded as "Alida Van Schaick." Even if the brother, Hendrick, in his Bible record, made such an omission, it is highly unlikely that the church record would say "Margaretje, daughter of Maria Roseboom," and not "Robert Lansing's wife." Therefore we reason that the Margaret whom Lansing married was one or other of two cousins of this Margaret, of the same name, Hendrick's Margaret, born five years earlier, or the daughter of Johannes, a year younger. The church burials give a Maria Roseboom, interred July 10, 1741, which could be neither mother nor daughter, but a person apart.

Myndert died somewhat early, after a rather uneventful life holding the modest position of the youngest of the family. His sons, Hendrick and Johannes, or John, as the name began now to be spelled, the one named for Myndert's father, the other for his elder brother, brought up families and lived to ripe years; the mother, Maria, evidently being gifted with ability to manage her affairs well, notwithstanding her repeated afflictions. The Vinhagen family was one that appears often in the early records. The Calendar of Wills gives "Jan Vinhagen, elder in the Reformed church, 1684," but there is obscurity as to Maria's parentage. She may have been an unmentioned daughter of Jan Dirkse Vinhagen and his wife Maritje (Maria), and then would be a younger child with her mother's name, and born about 1688, or she may have lived somewhere out of Albany and been there married, which would account for much of the difficulty in the case.

CHILDREN.

1. *Hendrick Myndert,* b. Sept. 15, 1707; m. Maria Ten Eyck. (3)
2. *Maria,* b. Sep. 23, 1709; d. Dec. 16, 1722, ae. 13.
3. *Margaret,* b. Sep. 2, 1711; d. Apr. 6, 1741, ae. 29.
4. *Alida,* b. Sep. 1, 1713; m. Dec. 11, 1735, Sybrant G. Van Schaick; d. July 20, 1770, ae. 56.
5. *John,* b. Jan. 11, 1716; d. Apr. 11, 1783, ae. 67.

3. Mynheer HENDRICK MYNDERTSE ROSEBOOM, son of Myndert Roseboom and Maria Vinhagen, (2), was born in Albany, N. Y., Sept. 15, 1707. He and his sons, all three of whom were officers in the Old French war, and in the Revolution, were earnest, patriotic men, actively engaged in business enterprise, and interested in the development of the country, both by extending trade on the frontier and in promoting settlement of the virgin lands. His social position was excellent, his sister, Alida, having married Sybrant G. Van Schaick, the Mayor of the city, son of Gerrit Van Schaick, who was one of the patentees of the Cherry Valley grant of 8,000 acres at the head of the Susquehannah, the others being John Lindsey, Jacob Roseboom and Lendert Gansevoort, with whose family his grandaughter was to intermarry.

Sympathizing with those who had suffered, like his own ancestors, and as his children were to do again, from tyranny, when the band of Scotch-Irish pilgrim Puritans from Londonderry, N. H., in 1740, were making their way to the wilds of Lindsey's Bush, it was on his sloop that passage was given them up the Hudson river, and from his "stoor" of merchandise that they were succoured with implements and supplies for their undertaking. He had a strong band of sons, only one of whom, John, however, married. Myndert, the eldest, kept up the mercantile establishment at Albany, exporting furs, and receiving from Holland and England consignments of merchandise, including silverware, in which the traffic of the family with the Indians appears to have largely consisted. It is known that silver or pewter medals, bearing the image of the Virgin, were distributed by the French traders and Jesuit priests, and are occasionally found in the debris of the Indian settlements along the Mohawk. When Matthew Campbell, of Cherry Valley, returned as a boy from his captivity with the Indians, after the massacre of 1778, he was decorated with a small brooch set with a dozen flat diamonds, perhaps rifled from the body of some officer, and with two tiny ring buckles, half round, in silver, no doubt precisely such as are described in the dealings between Myndert Roseboom and his brother John, who established himself at Schenectady, in order to be in closer touch with the Indians of Niscayuna.

An account book is preserved by the family, inscribed "Rates of the Powder House; Hendrick Roseboom, 1775." From this relic it appears that from 1771 to 1786 he held the important and necessarily dangerous office of "Cruyt magassijn meester," i. e., master of the powder magazine, at Albany, in trust for, "Die Committie," —the Committee of Public Safety. For some years the deposits of ammunition in his care were small, his own son, Myndert, being among the first, apparently, to utilize the magazine; but as the great struggle of the war came on we find the old Dutch Magazijne-meester still in charge, and on one occasion loading up 25 wagons with no less than a hundred barrels, and delivering it into the hands of the military authorities, represented by Mr. Philip Van Rensselaer. Lead, buck-shot, swan-shot and flints were part of the "stoor" supplies.

Nearly 70 years old at the opening of the war, Mr. Hendrick Roseboom was unfit for service in the field, but he must have been still one of the efficient and trusted men of the community, to be continued in so vital a charge under such altered circumstances. The "rates," as appear from the first page of the gun powder book, were "4 shillings for every barrel, 3 shillings for every half barrel, 2 ditto for every quarter cask or lesser quantity." The following entries, written partly in Dutch by Mr. R. himself, and partly in a beautiful English hand, perhaps by his clerk, reveal the nature of the trust, and the names of some of the individuals concerned.

1771, Nov. 22. Myndert Roseboom, Dr.; to storage of 1 Barrel & 19 half ditto, Gun Powder. 1773, Oct. 27, Mindert ontfangen 5 Vatties van 100 lb. in stoor; i. e., Myndert (Roseboom, Dr.) received 5 kegs of 100 lbs. each, in store. 1773, Dec. 15, Aen* 5 Barrells Cruyt en Die Magessijn ontfangen; i. e., ditto. 5 Barrels of Powder received in the Magazine. The record gives powder stored for well known names, as Gerrit Jacob Lansingh, Hendrick Wendell, Peter Dox, Dannel Cambel, Hermanus Ten Eyck, etc. 1773, Oct. 27, Ontfangen Van Abraham Cuyler 10 Vatties van 50 per vat Cruyt in Die Magessijn gestort. 1775, Jan. 7, van Goesse van Schajeck entfangen in Magessijn 24 Cwartter (quarter) Vatties Cruyt. 1776, Aug. 8, 225 Powder, 500 Flints Kilyan Van Renselaer. 1776, July 1, Powder in Store out of the other Side from the Committee 43 cask of 50 lb. each, etc.. Delivard out of the Store of Commitee (by order to) Col. Lansing, Peter Van Ness, Dirk Jansen, Col. Van Renselaer, (Henry Kilyan), Anthony Van Bergen, Col. Van Den Bergh, Lt. S. J. Schyler etc., had dealings with the Magazine. 1777, June 10, 100 Barrells Loaded by order of Mr. Philip Van Renselaer 25 Waggons Each 4 Bar'l. This was out of the store of the Commitee. This large

---

* "Aen" seems to be a contraction for aenlyk, i. e., ditto. A vat or "vattie" was a cask; our word vat comes from the same word.

requisition of gunpowder was doubtless destined for the operations which ended in the surrender of Burgoyne, Oct. 17, 1777. in which Col. H. K. Van Renselaer participated Consignments of ammunition were also sent to Schenactady, Schohary, and to the friendly Indians at Onida.

He died in Canajoharie, N. Y., Apr. 23, 1803, aged 95. (1)

He married, Oct. 29, 1734, MARIA TEN EYCK, dau. of Barent Ten Eyck and Neeltje Schermerhooren. She was born in Albany, Apr. 26, 1708, and died there, May 9, 1790, aged 82.

CHILDREN.

1. *Myndert*, b. June 2, 1735; d. Apr. 10, 1806, ae. 70.
2. *Barent*, b. Oct. 29, 1736; d. Feb. 16, 1796, ae. 59. (m)
3. *John*, b. Oct. 23, 1739; m. Susannah Veeder. (4)
4. *Neeltie*, b. Nov. 20, 1741; m. Mar. 14, 1767, Jacob G. Lansing; d. May 6, 1770, ae. 28.
5. *Maria*, b. June 13, 1746; d. Jan. 24, 1781, ae. 34.

Col. MYNDERT ROSEBOOM, son of Hendrick M. Roseboom and Maria Ten Eyck, (3), was born in Albany, N. Y., June 2, 1735. Several interesting documents illustrate the military and patriotic record of this soldier of the French and Indian war, and of the Revolution. In the Calender of New York Historical Manuscripts is the following " Warrant, Apr. 23, 1759, in favor of Capt. Myndert Roseboom, for £1,487, being the amount of bounty and enlisting money for 111 volunteers." An original Order Book* of the year 1759, kept by Capt. Roseboom, who on May 16 signs himself Major, indicates that he was Adjutant or assistant Adj't. of that division of Gen. Amherst's army which that year, under Col. Prideaux, made an expedition against Fort Niagara, which it captured July 24–5. The book begins Apr. 13, with the troops at Albany, the orders being given by Col. Corsa, under Cols. " Pridieu," Johnson, (afterwards Sir William) and Bradstreet. Some of the regiments are, the 44th, L. Royals, late Forbeses, Inniskillings, Royal Highlanders. Abercrombie's, Mury's, Pardoe's, and four battalions of Royal Americans. Leaving Albany May 8, he is with the troops as

---

*This book was used in 1765 for invoices of hardware, and on Sept. 29th of that year for the rent-roll of " ye lands" of Geo. Clark esq., to Ye inhabitants of Cherry Valley," with numbers of the lots and amounts of rent, many of the names being familiar: — Edmiston, McConnell, Linn, Sam'l and Wm. Ferguson, Jno. Wells, McCollum, Thomson, Dixon, Ramsey, Spencer, Taus, Dunlap, James Campbell, Shankland, Hopkins, and Lottridge. In 1775 accounts of church money received and expended were entered in Dutch by persons not named.

they march through the Mohawk Valley, the supplies being carried in whale-boats and bateaux on the river, and reaching Oswego on June 27, where the book closes. It contains the daily orders, paroles, countersigns, number of men, equipment of officers and men, accounts of courts martial, etc.

In 1761 "Myndert Roseboom, Esquire," received from Hon'ble Cadwallader Colden, President of His Majesty's Council and Commander in Chief of the Province, his commission as Lieut. Colonel of Brewerton's regiment, of which he was placed in charge. (i). His service to the cause of the Revolution is shown by a volume of records eloquent of the distress caused by the war, inscribed "Receipt Book; Albany, 12th, August, 1777. Commissioners, Middle District, City and county of Albany. Signed, Myndert Roseboom, Thos. Bancker, (major), and George White." While the father was guarding and issuing ammunition for the war, the son was caring for the fugitive sufferers from the distresses of the times, gathered at Albany. The book is full of receipts for moneys paid to parties who furnished food and supplies to the "poor distressed people," and the "Refugees," extending from Sept. 16, 1777 to Apr. 2, 1778, of which the following are samples: "Received, Albany, 16th Oct., 1777, from Col. Myndert Roseboom, the sum of thirty shillings for three head of cattle which I have slaughtered for the poor distressed people, Jno. Padgett." "Received, Albany, 6th Oct., 1777, from Col. Roseboom, twenty-four pounds, six shillings, in full for six weight flour, 30-3 weight at thirty-four shillings for John Depeyster. D. P. Ten Eycke." "Received, Albany, 15th Feb., 1778, from Col. Roseboom, the sum of sixteen pounds in full for one ox for the use of the poor. Phi'p Schuyler." "Received, Albany, 2nd Feb., 1778, from Col. Roseboom, the sum of sixty pounds for 3,000 weight of flour. Hendrick Roseboom."

Col. Roseboom was a merchant extensively engaged at Albany, both before and after the war, apparently continuing his father's business, and in correspondence with his brother John, at Schenectady; his brother, Barent, being also established at Albany in the fur trade. Letters are preserved from a mercantile correspondent in London, a fur dealer, one of which, treating of some transactions with the brothers at Albany, dated in Sept., 1775, just before the war, ends as follows: "I feel very sensibly for the distressed situation of America, as well as for many individuals in this country, and wish for nothing so much as to see a reconciliation take place, but sorry I am to say, that there is not the smallest appearance of it. Amos Hayton." This regret at the needless conflict continued to its close, and points to a feeling among better-thinking people in the mother-country of which history takes little account; as witness another of these business epistles, dated at the close of the war, in 1781, which reveals how men were writhing with the utter demoralization of business in which they neither could pay their creditors nor dare give credit, and ending with these strong words: "You may believe me when I assure you that I rejoice as sincerely as you can do at an end being put to the war with America, as I ever thought it both impolitick and unjust, and God knows I have suffered enough by it in being kept out of many sums of Money which has been owing me for several years past, but which I hope I may now soon receive or at least some part of them. I remain, &c., Amos Hayton."

This debtor could not pay, like others, who either defaulted or paid in worthless Continental notes, and Col. Roseboom bent to the storm and assigned his large affairs to his brother John and nephew Henry.

A copy of a deed (j) from Col. John Harper to Col. John Myndert Roseboom, dated Feb. 1, 1775, conveying lot No. Two of the Beaver Dam farm, is in possession of the family, and also one (k) conveying lot No. One, of the same farm to John Roseboom, brother of Myndert, dated Mar. 12, 1795, each of 250 acres. Another deed, dated Sept. 10, 1803, conveys a tract of 150 acres, adjoining the above, to Barent Roseboom, son of John. The lands afterwards in possession of the family were much more extensive than these three deeds indicate, and the tradition that Col. Roseboom received a grant from the government for military services is borne out by the following paper entitled "Accounts Current," "Col. Myndert Roseboom, with Barent Roseboom & Brothers, dated Canajoharie, May 6, 1805." Among these accounts is found the following item: "Dec. 26, 1799, paid Col. Campbell for three years' board, seventy-four pounds, fifteen shillings." This item shows that Col. Roseboom was a resident of Cherry Valley for three years, sometime previous to Dec., 1799, and we may fairly infer that the tradition regarding Government grants is not without foundation. He also acted as agent for the lands of Lieut. Governor George Clark. He died unmarried in Canajoharie, Apr. 10, 1806, aged 70.

---

4. Lieut. JOHN ROSEBOOM, son of Henrick M. Roseboom and Maria Ten Eyck, (3), was born in Albany, N. Y., Oct. 23, 1739. He was sometimes called John II., "Silversmith." He settled early at Schenectady as a merchant; his house, purchased in 1764, being on the northeast corner at the crossing of the road to the Fort and that to Niscayuna, the deed of which is extant. His business accounts from 1772 to 1789 are also preserved, and indicate that his dealings, besides general merchandise, were largely in silver ornaments which were bartered to those trading with the Indians, therefor being received furs and leather which were forwarded to his brother Myndert at Albany for shipment to London. One or two of the entries will illustrate the traffic: "Messrs. Abr. Van Epes & Jacob Van Epes; 5 arm bands, 3 round moons, 4 pare rist bands, 1 box, 50 pare Eare rings, 13 pare large, 100 broaches, 50 Doo. small—£21, 18, 0." In Apr., 1773, Gereet Teller & Will'm Groesbeek purchase such jewelry.—" care wheels, large crosses, half-moons, hare plaits," (perhaps like what the Dutch peasant-girls wear). " and 1 thousand gun-flints, to the amount of £115, 9, 0." "Myndert Roseboom in Albany" is debited, Nov., 1774, with an invoice amounting to £210, 17, 2, enumerating " 1368 lbs. of read Lether at 2s. 9d. per lb., 33 of parchment, 16 Otters, 1 Fisher, 14 Mush Ratts, 13 gray Skins, 9 Bare skins, 5 Beaver, etc." Apr. 14, 1786, John pays a bill " To Doc't Will'm Adams, for attending in my family as Docktor, £9, 10."

Mr. Roseboom was a member of the Committee of Safety and a Lieutenant in the army of the Revolution. On May 6, 1775, on the approach of the war, the freeholders and inhabitants of Schenectady at a meeting unanimously chose ten persons, of whom he was one, " to be a Committee of correspondence, safety and protection for the township," two of the others being James Wilson and Hugh Mitchell. These two men had retired from Cherry Valley before the oncoming of trouble, to Schenectady, the latter afterwards returning there to become the centre of one of the most harrowing episodes of the Massacre. His family were ruthlessly slain before his eyes, he indentifying the murderer in one of his Tory neighbors, named Newberry, whose hanging he subsequently procured. Wilson was surveyor-general of the county of Albany.

The Archives of the Militia and Roster of State troops, under date June 20, 1776, give John Roseboom as First Lieutenant of Capt. Oothout's, formerly Fonda's and Wasson's, company, in the Second, Col. Abm. Wemple's, regiment. The minutes of the Committee of Safety, June 2, 1779, indicate that Lieut. Roseboom was as yet serving at home, as he is at that date named with three others as salt commissioners. The meetings of the Committee were held in the house of William White, at Church and Front streets. Their extensive and multiform duties included the raising of troops, and all the details of military matters, and also the decision as judges in cases of those charged with treasonable sentiments or with being unfriendly to the cause of the colonies, or who had in any way been proved to have acted as allies of England. We can understand how ready these men were to avenge the blood of the family of one of their own number.

While a resident of Schenectady Mr. Roseboom went to Detroit, Mich., to trade with the Indians, making the first part of the journey in boats on the Mohawk river. Six weeks were consumed by this trip. Sometime previous to 1790 he moved from Schenectady and settled on the late Abram N. Van Alstine place, one mile east of Canajoharie Village. On this farm there was a private burial ground in which the following members of the family were interred: Hendrick M. Roseboom and his sons Myndert, Barent and John; Maria, dau. of John, his son Barent J., with his wife Sarah, and infant dau., and a grandson Peter Gansevoort. These nine were afterwards, about 1850, moved to Prospect Hill cemetery, Canjoharie. More recently Mrs. Susannah Roseboom and her son Myndert were moved from Schenectady, and another son, Henry, from Albany, and placed beside the others.

John Roseboom left at his death 2244 acres of land in Cherry Valley, embracing the Beaver Dam property, (j), which had previously been owned by Col. John Harper, and on which was a saw mill where, according to the journal of Lieut. William McKinstry, the timber was cut for the "block-house at the Fort." Most of this land though sold came back to his sons. He had also 708 acres in Oswego, 750 in the Sackindaga patent, as well as land in

Canajoharie, and several pieces of property in Albany. The latter included "two acres on Albany Hill," a house in State street for years occupied by Killien Killiense Van Rensclaer, and a "stoor" and lot in Market street. The transfer papers of his home in Schenectady give his name as "John H.," the initial of Hendrick, his father's name, being inserted for better identification, as was customary. For this property, so early as 1764, he paid £430 to Rich'd Collins, who the year previous had bought it of Thos. Nickson for £619, 7, 7. He died in Canajoharie, Apr. 4, 1805, aged 65.

He married, May 19, 1763, SUSANNAH VEEDER, dau. of Myndert Veeder and Elizabeth Douw. She was born in Scenectady, Apr. 18, 1744. She was descended from Simon Volkertse Veeder, "de bakker," born in 1624, settled in New Amsterdam in 1652, sold lot in 1654 for thirty beavers, moved to Beverwyck; owned land on the Normanskill; moved to Schnectady in 1662; owned a "bouwery" on the great flat there, numbered 9, containing 24 morgens*, and a village lot on the north corner of State and Ferry streets. He was the first of the name in America, and had four sons who left families, and also three daughters. Johannes Simonse Veeder, of Albany, third son of the above, had land on the Normanskill below Albany. He married, 1st, Nov. 19, 1697, Susanna, dau. of Myndert Wemple, who was the mother of Myndert Veeder and five others; he married, 2nd, June 3, 1718, Susanna Wendell, of Albany, and had one child. Myndert Veeder, of Albany, bap. there, Apr. 30, 1707, son of the above, married, Dec. 19, 1733, Elizabeth Douw, dau. of Volkert Douw and Margareta Van Tricht, of Rensselaerwyck Manor.

On her mother's side, the first ancestor in America was Capt. Volkert Janse Douw, from Frederickstadt, was in Beverwyck from 1638 to 1686; his house lot was on the west corner of State street and Broadway. He was a trader and brewer, and dealt largely in real estate. He married, in New Amsterdam, Apr. 19, 1650, Dorotee Janse, from Breestede, Holland. (She was a sister of Rutger Jacobson's wife, and died Nov. 22, 1781.) Volkert Douw, of Manor Rensselaerwyck, son of the above, married, Nov. 16, 1701, Margareta Van Tricht, who was buried Jan., 1752; he was buried Sept. 2, 1753. Elizabeth, their fourth child, bap. Oct. 24, 1711, married Myndert Veeder.

---

* A morgen contained 9722 square yards, or a little more than two acres.

After the death of her husband, Susannah Roseboom remained with her sons until the death of Barent in 1807, when she returned to Schenectady to pass the remaining days of life in her native place, where she died Jan. 26, 1812, aged 67.

CHILDREN.

1. *Hendrick,* b. Sept. 15, 1764; d. Apr. 21, 1790, ae. 25.
2. *Myndert,* b. July 29, 1766; d. Feb. 5, 1788, ae. 21.
3. *Elizabeth,* b. Dec. 25, 1768; m. Conrad Gansevoort. (11)
4. *Barent,* b. June 17, 1771; m. Sarah Schermerhorn; Catharine Tyms. (32)
5. *John J.,* b. Oct. 25, 1774; d. Mar. 15, 1829, ae. 54.
6. *Abraham,* b. Aug. 10, 1777; m. Ruth Johnson. (33)
7. *Maria,* b. Feb. 21, 1783; d. Apr. 16, 1796, ae. 13.

THE JOHNSONS.

5. The first American settler of the Johnson family was Capt. JOHN JOHNSON, who probably came from England in the fleet with John Winthrop, who arrived in Salem, Mass., June 22, 1630. He brought his wife and five children with him. He was most likely born prior to 1600, as his eldest son married in 1637. He settled in Roxbury, Mass., where he was chosen constable Oct. 19, 1630, and was made a freeman May 18, 1631. He was one of the founders of the church in July, 1632, of which Rev. John Eliot was the first pastor, and was one of the embryo parliament of that year. He was a deputy at the first general court in 1634 and for fifteen years afterwards, and became a member of the Ancient and Honorable Artillery Company in 1638, was clerk of that company for three years, and surveyor general of all the arms and amunition.

When Anne Hutchinson was taken into custody in 1637, the general court ordered that the arms of her Roxbury adherents be delivered to "goodman" Johnson, the town of Roxbury being required to take order for their custody and " if any charge arise to be defrayed by her husband." Capt. Johnson was a "very industrious and faithful man in his place," kept a tavern in Roxbury street where many public meetings were held, and was a man of great esteem and influence. On Feb. 6, 1645, this tavern with all the outbuildings was burned, with seventeen barrels of powder and other amunition which were stored there, the explosion shaking the houses in Boston and Cambridge as with an earthquake. At this fire the first book of records of the town of Roxbury, and the school charter were destroyed, the former was an irreparable loss.

"In answer to the petition of Barnabas Fawer's executors & ouseers of his last will & testament, liberty is graunted for a devision of the estate which the sd testator left to his wife & sonne Eliazur, & that the howse, prised at £180, shalbe estated on his sd son, & the other howse, prised at £40, shalbe estated on John Johnson, husband of Grace Fawer, the late wife of the foresd Barnabas & that the rest of the estate be equally devided so as to make the two whole pts equall between the mother & the son according to the will."

"This Court, taking notice of the contynuall paynes & faythfull endevours of Mr. Joh Johnson in the place of the surveyor generall, lookinge to the country armes & peurcinge many of the country debts, judge it meete he should have due recompence, & doe therefore order, that he shalbe allowed five poundes p annu, & to begin from the time of the Courte's last allowance to him for his paynes in that imployment."

On May 6, 1657, the court decreed that "Mr. John Johnson, having bin long serviceable in the place of surveyor gen'll, for which he hath never had any satisfaction, which this Court considering of, thinkes meet to graunt him 300 acors in any place where he can find it, according to law." He died in Roxbury, Sept. 30, 1659.

The following is an extract from his will:

"The last will & Testament of John Johnson of Roxbury, this 30th of the 7th, '59, having my perfect memory & understanding by the blessing of my mercyfull Father, whose reconciled face in Jesus Christ my soule waiteth to behould. I dispose of my worldly goods & estate as followeth. My dwelling house & certaine lands I have allready given to my beloved wife during the terme of her natural life, according to a deed wh is extant wh deede my will is shall be fulfilled, wherein also I have given her £60 for her houschould furniture, wh house & lands after my wives decease I give unto my 5 children to be equally divided, my eldest sonne having a double portion therein, according to the word of God. * * * * also I make my sonns Isaak Johnson & Robert Pepper my executors of this my last will & Testament, & I request my deare brethren Elder Heath, & Deakon Parke, to be overseers, of this my will & Testament, & in token of my love I give ym each £10. If my children should disagree in any thing, I doe order them to choose one man more, to these my overseers, & stand to theire determination."

An inventorie of ye goods and chattell of John Johnson Late of Roxbery Deceased:

	£	s	d
2 fether beads 2 bolsters 3 pilows 2 sheets wh (with) 3 blankets and A rugg with curtans and valents (valences) with a bed steed	10	00	00
a tabl 6 Joyn stools and a carpet	2	00	00
1 drincking glass 1 hoar (hour) glass	00	01	06
3 hats & wearing aparell wth boots stockings bands caps handcherches	20	00	00
2 bibls 1 psalme booke and 8 books more	01	05	00
12lb of yarn 13 scains	01	04	00
1 curtain rod 1 pair of pinsers 2 pair of sheers	00	03	06
8 silver spoons	02	00	00

He married, 1st, MARGERY, who died June 9, 1655, in Roxbury. (Nothing more regarding her can be ascertained.)

He married, 2nd, GRACE FAWER*, born Negus, and widow of Barnabas Fawer. She died after 1659.

CHILDREN: by the first marriage.

1. *Isaac*, m. Jan. 20, 1637, Elizabeth Porter. (6)
2. *Humphrey*, m. Mar. 20, 1643, Ellen Cheney.
3. *Mary*, m. Roger Mowry; d. Jan., 1679; he d. Jan. 5, [1666.
4. *Elizabeth*, m. Mar. 14, 1643, Robert Pepper; d. Jan. 5, 1684; he d. July [7, 1684.
5. *A daughter.*

---

6. Capt. ISAAC JOHNSON, son of Capt. John and Margery Johnson, (5), was born in England, and came to Massachusetts with his parents in 1630. He was admitted to be a freeman Mar. 4, 1635, and became a member of the Roxbury church. He joined the Ancient and Honorable Artillery Company in 1645, was lieutenant in 1666 and its captain in 1667. He was ensign of the Roxbury company previous to 1653, and on June 13, of that year was elected captain. In 1671 he represented the town in the general court. "On July 6, 1675, a body of fifty-two Praying Indians, Rev. John Eliot's converts marched from Boston for Mount Hope under the intrepid Captain Isaac Johnson who afterwards certified that the most of them acquitted themselves courageously and faithfully."

---

* Grace Negus married, 1st, Mar. 10, 1643, Barnabas Fawer, who came from Dorchester, England, in 1635, and died Dec. 13, 1654.

CHILD.

Eleazar.

"Beside the troop of Prentice, Capt. Isaac Johnson was ordered on July 15, 1675, to march with soldiers listed under the order of Major Treatt, (Governor of Connecticut), as also some others from Boston, to relieve Mendon and Wrentham. Like all other train-band captains he was a man of distinguished social position."

"The Indian War of 1675-'76—'Philip's War,' as it is called,—was the severest ordeal through which New England was ever called upon to pass. The intrepid Capt. Isaac Johnson, of Roxbury, with five other captains, was killed while storming the Narragansett stronghold, when that fierce tribe was destroyed at the famous 'Fort Fight,' Dec. 19, 1675. The only entrance to the fort was over a felled tree, bridging the swamp, over which but one man could pass at a time, and this narrow pathway was protected by a blockhouse. The brave Roxbury captain was shot dead on this bridge, over which he was leading his men."

Following is his will:

The Last Will & testamt of Isaac Johnson of Roxbury this 8 of March 1673 I haveing my perfect memory & understanding first I committ my Soule to God in Jesus Christ. Secondly I committ my body to my beloved wife & children to be decently buried. Thirdly I doe dispose of my worldly goods as followeth — my debts & funerall charges being discharged my will is that Elizabeth my beloved wife Shall have all my moveable goods except my apparrell at her owne dispose & the houseing & Land during the time of her Naturall life & after her decease my will is the houseing & Land bee divided betweene my fower children my Sonne Isaac or his heires to have a double portion & Soe the portion of the rest to goe to theire heires that is in case my imediate Children any of them bee dead before they come to Injoy there portion. Also my will is that my Beloved wife bee Sole Executrixe of this my Last will & I request my Brother Edward Porter & Cozen John Weld to bee Overseerss of this my Last will my will is that all my wearcing apparell be divided betweene my sonne Isaac & my Sonne Nathaniell my Sonne Isaac to have two Shares or a double portion of my sd apparrell. Witness my hand this 28th of June One thousand Six hundred Seaventy five. Isaac Johnson Senior.

Mr. Jno Weld & Samuell Craft appeared before Symon Bradstreet Samuell Danforth & Edw Tyng Esqrs this 10th of febr 1676 made Oath that being well acquainted wth the Late Capt. Isaac Johnson & his hand writeing they verrily believe & Judge that the above sd whereto his name is Subscribed is all his owne hand writeing this thus deposed as Attests. ffreegrace Bendall, Recordr.

Inventory, £579, 12s, 6d. House, out-houses, orchard gardens, etc., 120. s.l.a., £365. 2 horses, 2 oxen, 4 cows, 4 young cattle, 7 swine, stack of bees, bridle, saddle, pillion, 3 bibles; carpenter, mason & wheelwright tools; and furnishings of a parlor, kitchen, parlor chamber, kitchen chamber, and cellar.

He married, Jan. 20, 1637, ELIZABETH PORTER, of Roxbury, who died, Aug. 13, 1683.

CHILDREN.

1. *Elizabeth,* b. Dec. 24, 1637; m. Dec. 20, 1658, Henry Bowen; d. Apr. 20, 1701, ae. 63.
2. *John,* b. Nov. 3, 1639; d. Dec. 18, 1661, ae. 22.
3. *Mary,* b. Apr. 24, 1642; m. Dec. 17, 1663, William Bartholomew; d. after 1697.
4. *Isaac, Jr.,* b. Nov. 7, 1643; m. Mary Harris. (7)
5. *Joseph,* b. Nov. 9, 1645; d. young.
6. *Nathaniel,* b. May 1, 1647; m. Apr. 29, 1667, Mary Smith; d. after 1697.

---

7. ISAAC JOHNSON, Jr., son of Capt. Isaac Johnson and Elizabeth Porter, (6), was born in Roxbury, Mass., Nov. 7, 1643. He moved to Middletown, Conn., where he was admitted to the church by letter from the church at Roxbury, Nov. 26, 1672. He died there, Feb. 23, 1720, aged 76.

He married, Dec. 26, 1669, MARY HARRIS, dau. of Daniel Harris and Mary Weld. She was born in Rowley, Mass., Feb. 2, 1651, and died in Middletown, Aug. 1, 1740, aged 89.

CHILDREN.

1. *Isaac,* b. Dec. 19, 1670.
2. *Daniel,* b. Oct. 8, 1672; m. Abigail Leek. (8)
3. *John,* b. Aug. 1, 1674; d. Jan. 6, 1693, ae. 18.
4. *Joseph,* b. Mar. 9, 1677.
5. *Nathaniel,* b. Jan. 17, 1679.
6. *Elizabeth,* b. Feb. 19, 1681.
7. *William,* b. Mar. 14, 1683; d. Mar. 25, 1683.
8. *Mary,* b. Jan. 18, 1687.
9. *Ebenezer,* b. Oct. 29, 1692; d. Oct. 31, 1692.

---

8. DANIEL JOHNSON, son of Isaac Johnson, Jr., and Mary Harris, (7), was born in Middletown, Conn., Oct. 8, 1672, and died there, Jan. 28, 1758, aged 85.

He married, Feb. 11., 1707, ABIGAIL LEEK, who was born in 1684, and died in Middletown, Oct. 12, 1757, aged 73.

CHILDREN.

1. *Abigail,* b. Dec. 8, 1707.
2. *Daniel, Jr.,* b. June 8, 1710; m. Elizabeth Ward; Jane Richardson; Edith Arnold; Sarah Tryon. (9)
3. *Mary,* b. May 4, 1713.
4. *Caleb,* b. July 27, 1717.

---

9. DANIEL JOHNSON, Jr., son of Daniel Johnson and Abigail Leek, (8), was born in Middletown, Conn., June 8, 1710.

He married, 1st, Oct. 17, 1734, ELIZABETH WARD, dau. of George Hubbard and Mehitable Miller, and widow of John Ward. She was baptized in Middletown, Apr. 22, 1711, and died there, July 28, 1746, aged 35.

He married, 2nd, Jan. 13, 1747, JANE RICHARDSON, who died in Middletown, Jan. 24, 1754, aged 36.

He married, 3rd, Nov. 14, 1754, EDITH ARNOLD, dau. of John Arnold and Edith Markham. She was baptized in Middletown, Nov. 8, 1713, and died there, Sept. 4, 1755, aged 41.

He married, 4th, Dec. 15, 1755, SARAH TRYON, dau. of Richard Goodrich and Hannah Bulckley, and widow of William Tryon. She was born in Middletown, July 6, 1715.

CHILDREN:— by the first marriage.

1. *Elizabeth,* b. Aug. 28, 1735.
2. *Daniel,* b. Oct. 8, 1737; d. Mar. 24, 1740, ae. 2.
3. *Daniel,* b. Jan. 9, 1741.
4. *Seth,* b. Sept. 6, 1743.
5. *Jesse,* b. Nov. 7, 1745; m. Mary Stevenson; Abigail Goodwin. (10)

CHILDREN:— by the second marriage.

6. *Lucretia,* b. Sept. 12, 1748.
7. *Jane,* b. Nov. 12, 1749.
8. *Abigail,* b. Dec. 2, 1751; m. May 30, 1771, Eliphlet Hubbard.
9. *A daughter,* b. Jan. 9, 1753; d. Jan. 10, 1753.

CHILD:— by the third marriage.

10. *A daughter,* b. and d. Aug. 19, 1755.

CHILDREN:— by the fourth marriage.

11. *Bulckley,* b. Feb. 24, 1758. } Twins.
12. *Edith,* b. Feb. 24, 1758. }

---

10. JESSE JOHNSON, son of Daniel Johnson, Jr., and Elizabeth Ward, (9), was born in Middletown, Conn., Nov. 7, 1745. He was a farmer, and the curing of beef for use at sea was also an im-

portant adjunct in his business life. He lived at Middletown and Chatham until 1804, when he considered it best to remove his two young sons from the temptation of following the sea, that had taken his eldest son so suddenly five years before, and which had proved fatal to so many of the young men of that locality. Through the influence and assistance of a fellow-townsman, Joseph White, M.D., who left Chatham on the completion of his medical course and in 1787 settled in Cherry Valley, N. Y., Mr. Johnson purchased a farm one and one-half miles south of that village, and built a house on it in the summer of 1804, and in November moved his family with all their worldly goods in wagons. He was elected elder of the Presbyterian church in 1814 and held that office during the remainder of his life. He was a consistant christian and a benevolent man. He died at his home, Apr. 30, 1832, aged 86.

He married, 1st, Feb. 27, 1769, MARY STEVENSON, dau. of John Stevenson and Susanna Savage. She was born in Middletown, Mar. 14, 1747, and died in the town of Cherry Valley, Nov. 23, 1809, aged 62.

He married, 2nd, Mar., 1812, ABIGAIL GOODWIN,* born Butler, widow of Samuel Goodwin, Jr. She was born Oct., 1751. After Mr. Johnson's death she returned to Madison, N. Y., and lived with her son, Samuel Goodwin, Jr., where she died Oct. 31, 1834, aged 83.

CHILDREN; — by the first marriage.

1.	Robert,	b. Aug. 9, 1769;	m. Lucy Wilcox.	(50)
2.	Jesse,	b. July 12, 1771;	d. Oct. 11, 1775, ae. 4.	
3.	Elizabeth,	b. June 18, 1773;	m. Samuel Stewart, Jr.	(59)
4.	Mary,	b. May 17, 1775;	m. Col. Eli Wilder.	(73)
5.	Jesse,	b. Apr. 9, 1777;	d. Mar. 29, 1780, ae. nearly 3.	
6.	Ruth,	b. Mar. 14, 1779;	m. Abraham Roseboom.	(33)
7.	Lucy,	b. May 3, 1781;	m. Dr. James Kennedy.	(105)
8.	Sally Maria,	b. Sept. 13, 1783;	m. Dr. Ebenezer Johnson.	(106)
9.	Erastus,	b. Apr. 10, 1786;	m. Jerusha W. Holt.	(115)
10.	Jesse,	b. May 23, 1792;	d. May 19, 1813, ae. nearly 21.	

---

* Abigail Butler married, 1st, Jan. 18, 1781, Samuel Goodwin, Jr., son of Samuel Goodwin and Laodamia Merrill. He was born in Hartford, Conn., Oct. 7, 1752, and died there, Apr. 6, 1807, aged 54.

CHILD.

Samuel, Jr., b. Dec. 8, 1781; m. Feb. 24, 1805, Abigail Olcott; Oct. 8, 1846, Rebecca Forbes Bacon; d. May 22, 1852, ae. 70

ELIZABETH ROSEBOOM GANSEVOORT AND DESCENDANTS.

11. ELIZABETH ROSEBOOM, dau. of John Roseboom and Susanna Veeder, (4), was born in Schenectady, N. Y., Dec. 25, 1768. Her early life was spent in Albany, but her father's family moved to Canajoharie previous to her marriage in 1791. "Many years before her death her husband removed to Schenectady and soon after to Albany, where she resided amid the scenes of her early associations, till not long before her decease. The last few years of her life were spent with her daughter, Mrs. Cooke, in Holmdel, N. J. Possessed of a strong mind, unostentatious in her manners, firm and decided in her character, dignified in her deportment, and withal benevolent and kind, she endeared herself to a large circle of friends. She was for many years a member of the North Dutch Church of Albany and her christian deportment was consistent and steady. A life that has been spread over so large space of time cannot depart without making us feel that we have been further removed than ever from the scenes of the past. We no longer hear the venerable matron of more than four-score describe the manners of those days of simplicity, nor hear an eye-witness relate the events of those interesting times. It was during those years of her life that the mind receives its most vivid impressions to which it reverts with most interest, that the stormy seasons of the American Revolution occurred. Her memory had treasured up many interesting incidents of those times." The writer remembers hearing her narrate an incident that occurred in her early days: Gen. Burgoyne

had boasted that he would make elbow-room as he came down from Canada, and as he was brought to Albany after his surrender, a crazy fellow stepped in ahead of the procession and wagging his elbows, shouting "elbow-room, elbow-room for Burgoyne!" She died in Holmdel, Jan. 11, 1850, aged 81.

She married, Nov. 12, 1791, CONRAD GANSEVOORT, son of Dr. Peter Gansevoort, and Garritje Ten Eyck. He was born in Albany, Mar. 28, 1761. He was a direct descendant of John Wessel Gansevoort (Wesselus Gansefortius) who was born in Gronigen, Holland, in 1419 and died in 1489. The latter was known as Wessel, and was also called "Lux Mundi,"—light of the world. He was an intimate friend of Thomas à Kempis, as well as of Sixtus IV. Soon after the latter was made Pope in 1471, he asked Gansevoort what he could do for him, whereupon Wessel asked for a Greek and Hebrew Bible from the Vatican library. "You shall have it," said the Pope, "but what a simpleton you are! why did you not ask me for a bishopric?" "Because I do not want it," was the simple reply. His descendant, Harmen Harmense VanGansevoort, came to America and was a brewer in Beverwyck (Albany) in 1660, and died July 23, 1710. His son Leendert (Leonard) who was born in 1681 and died in 1763 was the father of Dr. Peter Gansevoort, born in 1725, and died in 1809.

Conrad Gansevoort, was a member of Isaac DeForrest's company, in the regiment of Col. Jacob Lansing, Jr., first Albany county militia, raised in the city and commissioned Oct. 20, 1775. On Mar. 3, 1780, he was made ensign of the company, Garrit Groesbeck becoming captain in place of DeForrest, and on June 20 he was made second lieutenant. After the close of the war he established himself in the mercantile business in the town of Minden, Montgomery county, and erected a dwelling with a store in it on a knoll at the foot of Sand Hill. He was a man much respected, and after years of successful trading he retired from business and returned to Schenectady about 1812, and subsequently to Albany— probably about 1816. "The Reformed Dutch Church of Canajoharie was erected on Sand Hill in 1750, nearly a mile to the westward of Fort Plain. The merchant, Conrad Gansevoort, had the only cushioned pew in it." He died while on a visit in Bath, N. Y., Aug. 9, 1829, aged 68.

CHILDREN.

1.	*Peter Conrad,*	b. Aug. 7, 1792;	d. July 25, 1794, ae. 2.		
2.	*Peter Conrad,*	b. Aug. 6, 1794;	d. June 7, 1829, ae. 34.		
3.	*Maria,*	b. June 20, 1796;	m. Rev. Samuel A. VanVranken.	(12)
4.	*John Roseboom,*	b. Aug. 27, 1798;	m. Rebecca Irwin.	(13)
5.	*Henry,*	b. Dec. 25, 1800;	d. May 29, 1831, ae. 30.	
6.	*Ten Eyck,*	b. Jan. 5, 1803;	m. Helen R. Lyon.	(14)
7.	*Susan,*	b. Mar. 19, 1805;	m. Dr. Robert W. Cooke.	(15)
8.	*Catherine Elizabeth,*	b. June 18, 1810;	m. Ambrose W. Cooke; John V. S. [Hazard.	(16)

---

12. MARIA GANSEVOORT dau. of Conrad Gansevoort and Elizabeth Roseboom, (11), was born in Fort Plain, N. Y., June 20, 1796, and died in Freehold, N. J., June 1, 1831, aged nearly 35.

She married, Oct. 13, 1817, Rev. SAMUEL ALEXANDER VAN VRANKEN, D. D.,* son of Nicholas VanVranken and Ruth Comstock. He was born in Fishkill, N. Y., Feb. 20, 1792. He was a Professor in Rutgers College and Theological Seminary, in New Brunswick, N. J., where he died, Jan. 1, 1861, aged 68.

CHILDREN.

1.	*Nicholas,*	b. 1818;	d. Mar. 2, 1856, ae. 38.	
2.	*Gansevoort,*	b. Dec. 2, 1820;	m. Mary C. Brinckerhoff.	(17)
3.	*Elizabeth Gansevoort,*	b. 1822;	d. Nov. 5, 1839, ae. 17.	
4.	*Maria Gansevoort,*	b. 1824;	d. Aug. 27, 1843, ae. 19.	
5.	*John Mabon,*	b. Feb. 18, 1827;	d. Apr. 13, 1829, ae. 2.	

---

13. JOHN ROSEBOOM GANSEVOORT, son of Conrad Gansevoort and Elizabeth Roseboom, (11), was born in the town of Minden, N. Y., Aug. 27, 1798. He was educated in Albany, left there in 1817, and was one of the early pioneers settlers in Bath, N. Y. He was an extensive merchant and forwarder of produce, when the

---

* Rev. S. A.Van Vranken married, 2nd, May 6, 1835, Maria Swift, dau. of Henry Swift and Rebekah Warner. She was born in Poughkeepsie, N. Y., Sept. 22, 1814, and died there, June, 2, 1841, aged 26.

CHILDREN.

1. *Frances,* b. Jan. 28, 1836; m. May 23, 1860, Rev. John McClellen Holmes; d. Oct. 30, 1874, ae. 38.
2. *Samuel Alexander,* b. Aug. 5, 1840; d. Dec. 1, 1844, ae. 4.

He married, 3rd, Dec. 18, 1851, Mary B. Boulden, dau. of Thomas Bond and Jane Maffett and widow of John Ford, and Nathan Boulden. She was born in New Castle, Del., Nov. 25, 1805.

chief highway to the Atlantic was down the Susquehanna river. He was an active Mason and one of the charter members who re-established Steuben Lodge, No. 112, F. & A. M., in Bath, in 1846. He died there, May 19, 1856, aged 57.

He married, Dec. 7, 1820, REBECCA IRWIN, dau. of Jared Irwin and Lucretia Patterson. She was born in Dansville, N. Y., Dec. 29, 1805, and died in Bath, May 6, 1887, aged 81.

CHILDREN.

1.	Elizabeth,	b. Oct. 28, 1821;	m. Henry A. Ogden.		(18)
2.	James,	b. Nov. 10, 1823;	m. Eliza Ogden.		(19)
3.	Peter Conrad,	b. Dec. 4, 1825;	d. May 31, 1856, ae. 30; drowned at [Cincinnati, O.		
4.	Susan Catherine,	b. Apr. 23, 1828;	d. July 1, 1832, ae. 4.		
5.	Mary Lucretia,	b. June 23, 1830;	m. Edward Howell, Jr.; Hiram R. [Hess.		(20)
6.	Henry Martin,	b. Apr. 14, 1832;	d. Dec. 4, 1833, ae. 1.		
7.	Robert Hubbard,	b. Dec. 7, 1834;	d. Apr. 16, 1887, ae. 52.		
8.	Helen Maria,	b. Oct. 14, 1838;	m. William W. Allen.		(21)

---

14. Dr. TENEYCK GANSEVOORT, son of Conrad Gansevoort and Elizabeth Roseboom, (11), was born in the town of Minden, N. Y., Jan. 5, 1803. He graduated with distinction from Union college in 1822, and afterwards at the Medical college in Philadelphia. In 1824 he settled in Bath, N. Y., and practiced with success. He subsequently engaged extensively in mercantile pursuits. Liberality and generosity were marked traits of this upright man, kind and benevolent neighbor, and devoted husband, father and friend. He died suddenly in Bath, Sept. 25, 1842, aged 39.

He married, Oct. 14, 1828, HELEN REYNETTE LYON, dau. of Moses Lyon and Elizabeth Arnett. She was born in Prattsburg, N. Y., Feb. 4, 1811, and died near Wilson, N. C., while returning from Florida, Apr. 21, 1880, aged 69.

CHILDREN.

1.	Catherine Elizabeth,	b. Aug. 1, 1833;	m. Duncan S. Magee; Benj. F. [Angel.	(22)
2.	Conrad,	b. Jan. 6, 1836;	m. Cornelia M. Fenn.	(23)
3.	Mary Woods,	b. May 19, 1839;	m. John N. Hungerford.	(24)
4.	TenEyck,	b. Aug. 18, 1842;	d. Oct. 8, 1867, ae. 25.	

15. SUSAN GANSEVOORT, dau. of Conrad Gansevoort and Elizabeth Roseboom, (11), was born in Minden, N. Y., Mar. 19, 1805. By her earnest life, steadfast faith and self-sacrificing endeavor she endeared herself to all with whom she came in touch. She died in Holmdel, N. J., Nov. 21, 1894, aged 89.

She married, Sept. 22, 1830, Dr. ROBERT WOODRUFF COOKE, son of Dr. Ambrose Ellis Cooke and Sarah Pearsall Wheeler. He was born in Newton, N. J., Jan. 21, 1797. He graduated at the College of Physicians and Surgeons in New York, and in 1820 established himself in Holmdel, where he spent the remaining years of his life in untiring medical labor. Of his skill and success his numerous patrons bore witness in the extended practice they gave him during so many years. He died in Holmdel, Dec. 27, 1867, aged 70.

CHILDREN.

1. *Sarah Elizabeth*, b. Dec. 16, 1831; d. Apr. 16, 1867, ae. 35.
2. *Henry Gansevoort*, b. Feb. 3, 1833; m. Maria B. Cowdrey, (25)
3. *Ambrose Wheeler*, b. Nov. 23, 1834; is a farmer near Holmdel.
4. *Robert Woodruff*, b. Dec. 19, 1837; m. Hulda H. Van Mater. (26)
5. *Conrad Gansevoort*, b. Mar. 5, 1843; d. Apr. 26, 1844, ae 1.

16. CATHERINE ELIZABETH GANSEVOORT, dau. of Conrad Gansevoort and Elizabeth Roseboom, (11), was born in Minden, N. Y., June 18, 1810, and died in New York City, Apr. 5, 1884, aged 73.

She married, 1st, in 1832, AMBROSE WHEELER COOKE, son of Dr. Ambrose Ellis Cooke and Sarah Pearsall Wheeler. He was born in Bound Brook, N. J., Sept. 9, 1809, and died in Holmdel, N. J., May 9, 1833, aged 23, leaving no children.

She married, 2nd, Sept. 20, 1837, JOHN VAN SCHOONHOVEN HAZARD, son of John Hazard and Anna Van Schoonhoven. He was born in Westport, (in a part then called Compo), Conn., Sept. 20, 1802. In 1804 the family removed to Waterford, N. Y., and when of age he went to Albany and engaged in mercantile business. During the visit of Gen. LaFayette to this country in 1824–5, Mr. Hazard formed one of a party of military officers who escorted him from the Capitol in Albany to the Massachusetts state line. In 1840 he returned to Waterford, and remained there until about 1849, when he went to New York, and was with the firm of Myers & Co., and later with A. T. Stewart & Co. He retired from business in 1878, and moved to Brooklyn, in 1887, where he died, Feb. 26, 1893, aged 90.

CHILDREN:— by the second marriage.

1. *Elizabeth Gansevoort,* b. July 7, 1838; m. Gerrard Allen. (27)
2. *Anna Van Schoonhoven,* b. Dec. 9, 1839; resides in Brooklyn.
3. *John Wendell,* b. Oct. 26, 1841.
4. *Mary Allen,* b. June 14, 1843; d. May 2, 1844.
5. *Catherine Gansevoort,* b. May 4, 1846; d. Jan. 9, 1851, ae. 4.

---

17. GANSEVOORT VAN VRANKEN, son of Rev. Samuel A. Van Vranken and Maria Gansevoort, (12), was born in Holmdel, N. J., Dec. 2, 1820. He was educated at the Albany Academy and then engaged in mercantile pursuits in New York City until his illness prevented. He died in Hackensack, N. J., June 6, 1856, aged 35.

He married, Mar. 4, 1852, MARY CORNELIA BRINCKERHOFF,* dau. of Albert A. Brinckerhoff and Altia Hopper. She was born in Hackensack, Apr. 6, 1828. She resides in Elizabeth, N. J.

CHILD.

Mary Gansevoort, b. Dec. 14, 1852.

---

18. ELIZABETH GANSEVOORT, dau. of John R. Gansevoort and Rebecca Irwin, (13) was born in Bath, N. Y., Oct. 28, 1821, and died there, Dec. 14, 1862, aged 41.

She married, Aug. 20, 1844, HENRY AUSTIN OGDEN, son of Henry Ogden and Julia Livingston Peck. He was born in Unadilla, N. Y., Aug. 17, 1813. He was merchant in Cincinnati, Ohio, but failing health compelled him to leave a prosperous business and seek a warmer climate. He spent some time at Key West, Fla., where he was suttler in the army. Disappointed, he returned north to spend his remaining days with friends and relatives in Bath. Though he had much to attach him to life, he had lived long enough

---

* Mrs. Van Vranken married, 2nd, Jan. 28, 1863, Dr. Henry Rutgers Cannon, son of James Spencer Cannon and Katharine Brevoort. He was born in the township of Franklin, N. J., May 20, 1821.

CHILDREN.

1. *Henry Brevoort,* b. May 2, 1865.
2. *Bessie Duncan,* b. Aug 31, 1867; m. Jan. 21, 1891, De Witt Clinton Jones, Jr.

to learn its vanity, and so sought Him in whom death is disarmed of its terrors. He died in Bath, Aug. 30, 1853, aged 40.

CHILD.

Henry Gansevoort, b. Aug. 5, 1852.

---

19. JAMES GANSEVOORT, son of John R. Gansevoort and Rebecca Irwin, (13), was born in Bath, N. Y., Nov. 10, 1823. He was admitted an attorney in the N. Y. State Supreme Court at Albany, in Jan., 1847, was U. S. Deputy Marshall of the Census in 1850, and Postmaster of Bath in 1852. Then he was engaged in the mercantile business until 1872, when he went to California and lives in Alameda.

He married, Nov. 10, 1862, ELIZA OGDEN,* dau. of Gustavus Loomis and Julia Mix, and widow of Edmund Augustus Ogden. She was born in New York City, May 8, 1818.

---

20. MARY LUCRETIA GANSEVOORT, dau. of John R. Gansevoort and Rebecca Irwin, (13), was born in Bath, N. Y., June 23, 1830, and died there, June 24, 1895, aged 65.

She married, 1st, Sept. 18, 1850, EDWARD HOWELL, Jr., son of Edward Howell, and Hannah Cruger. He was born in Bath, Feb. 20, 1821. He studied law with his father, and was an attorney for the Erie railroad, and Secretary of the Buffalo, Corning and New York railroad when he died in Bath, Mar. 4, 1853, aged 32.

---

* Eliza Loomis married, 1st, May 28, 1835, Edmund Augustus Ogden, son of Henry Ogden and Julia Livingston Peck. He was born in Catskill, N. Y., July 20, 1811, and died in Fort Riley, Kan., Aug. 3, 1855, aged 44.

CHILDREN.

1. *Julia,* b. 1838; d. 1840.
2. *Henry Luddington,* b. 1840; d. 1858.
3. *Edmund Augustus,* b. 1842; d. 1868.
4. *Gustavus,* b. 1846; d. 1846.
5. *Eliza Emily,* b. June 28, 1848; m. Feb. 15, 1870, Thomas Cumming Clark; d. June 20, 1876, ae. nearly 28.
6. *Isabella,* b. Aug. 28, 1850.
7. *Kate Fauntleroy,* b. July 15, 1852; m. June 18, 1879, Edwin Browne Booth.
8. *Edith Panton,* b. July 19, 1854; d. June 13, 1890, ae. 35.

She married, 2nd, Jan. 16, 1862, HIRAM ROSS HESS,* son of Conrad Hess and Elizabeth Heckman. He was born in Bloomsburgh, Penn., Oct. 30, 1809. He engaged in mercantile pursuits in Philadelphia, and in 1834 moved to Bath, where he continued business. In 1846 he was appointed Loan Commissioner of the county, and in 1871 was elected Justice of the Peace; and in 1875 was re-elected to the latter office and served with credit for eight years. He died in Bath, Apr. 23, 1883, aged 73.

CHILDREN:— by the first marriage.
1. *Frances Minerva*,   b. Aug. 24, 1851; d. Dec. 7, 1851.
2. *Mary Edwardina*,   b. June 4, 1853; resides in Bath.

Capt. ROBERT HUBBARD GANSEVOORT, son of John R. Gansevoort and Rebecca Irwin, (13), was born in Bath, N. Y., Dec. 7, 1834. A student of medicine at Ann Arbor, Mich., when the war broke out he was made 2nd. Lieut. in Slocum's 1st. N. Y. Artillery, but when that battery was consolidated he resigned and enlisted in the afterwards famous 107th, at Elmira. From 1st. Lieut. of Company I, he was promoted Captain of Company G, "for bravery in the field and steady good conduct." Receiving their baptism of fire at Antietam, with his regiment he was present from that time till the war closed, at Chancellorville and Gettysburg, under Joe Hooker in the Atlanta campaign, and under Slocum from Atlanta to Savannah and from Savannah to the end. "And among those who upheld the honor of their regimental flag at all posts of duty, in camp and march, in siege and fight, Capt. Gansevoort was one of the foremost."

After recruiting his broken health at home, he settled in Milledgeville, Ga., but responding to a call for troops for Dakota, he proceeded to Fort Rice and served under Gen. Custer until 1874. He was hospital steward at Fort Rice, Fort Stephenson and Bismarck, when an injury by a fall from his horse compelled his resignation. For five years he held that position at the Soldiers' Home, at Bath,

---

* H. R. Hess married, 1st, June 8, 1835, Martha Powell, who was born in Philadelphia, Penn., Oct. 20, 1816, and died in Bath, Mar. 8, 1852, aged 35.

CHILDREN.
1. *Mary Elizabeth*,   b. July 27, 1836; d. Aug.   1856, ae. 20.
2. *George Powell*,   b. July 27, 1839; m. Ella Murray; d.
3. •*Margaret Augusta*, b. July 16, 1843; d. June 23, 1844, ae. nearly 1.

and was then promoted Adjutant, which he held until ill health required his resignation, Mar. 1.

Of splendid military mien this born soldier by his long service did honor to his Revolutionary ancestory, and to his descent through yet earlier generations, from the heroes and martyrs in the holy war waged by the Netherlanders against the cruelties of Spain, whose faith he shared. He died unmarried, in Bath, Apr. 16, 1887, aged 52.

21. HELEN MARIA GANSEVOORT, dau. of John R. Gansevoort and Rebecca Irwin, (13), was born in Bath, N. Y., Oct. 14, 1838.

She married, Oct. 30, 1861, WILLIAM W. ALLEN, son of John Thomas Allen and Minerva Ferris. He was born in the town of Howard, N. Y., Oct. 19, 1835. He is a great grandson of William Allen, of New England, who was active as a soldier in establishing American Independence. He was educated in Haverling academy, Bath, and in 1852 entered the banking house of Alfred Purdy Ferris, in that place, and was connected therewith until 1857, when the bank of Bath was organized of which he became teller. In 1863 it was made a National bank with Mr. Allen as cashier.

For many years he was treasurer of St. Thomas Church, of Haverling academy, and director and treasurer of the Urbana Wine Company. He was prominent in the creation of the Steuben Club, of Bath, a noted social organization of the county, and its first president, to which he was several times re-elected. He has always been active in politics but has never held public office, with the exception of commissioner of the U. S. Deposit Fund, for the county of Steuben, for fourteen years.

CHILDREN.

1. *Minerva Elizabeth*, b. Dec. 19, 1862; m. Edwin S. Underhill. (28)
2. *Gansevoort Irwin*, b. Dec. 1, 1867; lives in Bath.
3. *Walter Roseboom*, b. Jan. 4, 1871; lives in Bath.

22. CATHERINE ELIZABETH GANSEVOORT, dau. of Dr. TenEyck Gansevoort and Helen R. Lyon, (14), was born in Bath, N. Y., Aug. 1, 1833. She resides at Geneseo, N. Y.

She married, 1st, May 30, 1852, DUNCAN STEUART MAGEE, son

of John Magee and Arabella Orr Steuart. He was born in Bath, Nov. 29, 1831. He was associated with his father in business, and in 1851 they became interested in the Blossburg and Corning Railroad, and it was through their influence that the road was completed. He made his first purchase of coal lands in 1859, and opened the mines at Fall Brook, Penn., the same year. He died in Wiesbaden, Germany, May 8, 1869, aged 37.

She married, 2nd, Jan. 18, 1877, BENJAMIN FRANKLIN ANGEL,* son of Benjamin Angel and Abigail Stickney. He was born in Burlington, N. Y., Nov. 28, 1812. When a boy he went to Geneseo, and was educated at Temple Hill academy, studied law and was admitted to the Bar at the age of 19. In 1853 he was appointed Consul to Honolulu by President Pierce, and remained there about two years. He was then appointed Special Commissioner to China, to settle a dispute between some American merchants and the Chinese Government in regard to export duties. That successfully accomplished he returned home via East Indies, Egypt and Europe. During President Buchanan's administration he was appointed Minister to Norway and Sweden, serving there until he was retired in 1862. He died in Geneseo, Sept. 11, 1894, aged 81.

CHILDREN:—by the first marriage.
1. *Arabella Steuart*, b. Mar. 23, 1854; m. Alfred L. Edwards. (29)
2. *Helen Gansevoort*, b. Sept. 5, 1855; m. Lewis Edwards. (30)

---

23. CONRAD GANSEVOORT, son of Dr. TenEyck Gansevoort and Helen R. Lyon, (14), was born in Bath, N. Y., Jan. 6, 1836. In 1855 he went to Conneaut, Ohio, and engaged in mercantile business until May 15, 1861, when he enlisted as private in the 2nd. Ohio Battery. He was soon promoted to the rank of 2nd Lieut., and then to that of 1st Lieut. The Battery was placed under the command of Gen. J. C. Fremont at St. Louis, Mo., Aug., 1861, and during the famous "hundred days' campaign" in Missouri and

---

* B. F. Angel married, 1st, May 18, 1835, Julia Jones, dau. of Horatio Jones and Elizabeth Starr. She was born in the town of Geneseo, May 28, 1811, and died in New York City, Dec. 25, 1871, aged 60.

CHILDREN.
1. *Charles Henry*, b. Apr. 10, 1837; m. June 5, 1867, Sarah Dennay Smith.
2. *Franklin William* b. Dec. 2, 1840; m. Apr. 22, 1868, Marie Virginie Dessaint.
3. *Jenny Jones*, b. Oct. 29, 1844; m. Oct. 31, 1867, James Watson Gerard.

Arkansas, he saw hard service with Gen. Fremont and his successor, Gen. Asboth. He fought under Gen. Sigel at the battle of Pea Ridge. Ark., the most important and decisive victory of Sigel's campaign in the Southwest, on the 6th., 7th. and 8th. of Mar., 1862. On June 15, 1862, he was honorably discharged on account of physical disabilities, and returned to Conneaut and engaged in banking for several years. Then he held a position with the Fall Brook Coal Company, in Tioga county, Penn., for four years, and since 1874 has lived in Bath.

He married, Sept. 6, 1863, CORNELIA MARIA FENN, dau. of Philip Curtiss Fenn and Mary Tryon. She was born in Medina, Ohio. Oct. 8, 1833, and died in Rochester, N. Y., Oct. 24, 1887, aged 54, leaving no children. She was interred in Bath.

---

24. MARY WOODS GANSEVOORT, dau. of Dr. TenEyck Gansevoort and Helen R. Lyon, (14), was born in Bath, N. Y., May 19, 1839, and died in Corning, N. Y., Oct. 24, 1871, aged 32, leaving no children.

She married, June 22, 1859, JOHN NEWTON HUNGERFORD,* son of Lot Hungerford and Celinda Smith. He was born in Vernon, N. Y., Dec. 31, 1825. He was reared on a farm in Oneida county, and in 1846 graduated at Hamilton college. For many years he was engaged in mercantile business and banking in Corning, and in 1876 he was elected to the Forty-fifth Congress. Was a member of the Presbyterian church. He died in Corning, Apr. 2, 1883, aged 57.

---

25. Dr. HENRY GANSEVOORT COOKE, son of Dr. Robert W. Cooke and Susan Gansevoort, (15), was born in Holmdel, N. J., Feb. 3, 1833. He graduated from Rutgers College in 1853 with the degree of A. B., and received that of A. M. from the same institution on 1856. He took his degree of M. D. in 1857 from the college of Physicians and Surgeons in New York. He served as surgeon of the 29th New Jersey Volunteers with the "Army of the Potomac,"

---

* J. N. Hungerford married, 2nd, Oct. 18, 1881, Susan Medora Forrester, dau. of Daniel Aber and Susan Marsh, and widow of George R. Forrester. She was born in Bath, N. Y., Sept. 13, 1836.

and as a volunteer surgeon during the remainder of the war. He is a member of the District Medical Society of Monmouth county, of the State Medical Society and the American Medical Association. He practiced in Holmdel until the spring of 1897 when he moved to New Brunswick, N. J., where he continues his profession.

He married, June 8, 1876, MARIA BURRITT COWDREY, dau. of Peter Anderson Cowdrey and Maria Burritt. She was born in New York City, Jan. 6, 1844.

CHILDREN.

1. *Sara Elizabeth,* b. July 24, 1877.
2. *Maria Cowdrey,* b. Nov. 20, 1878.
3. *Robert Anderson,* b. Aug. 17, 1880.
4. *Susan Gansevoort,* b. June 4, 1882.
5. *Henry Gansevoort,* b. Sept. 12, 1883; d. Dec. 15, 1884, ae. 1.
6. *Edward Ambrose,* b. Apr. 22, 1887.

---

26. ROBERT WOODRUFF COOKE, son of Dr. Robert W. Cooke and Susan Gansevoort, (15), was born in Holmdel, N. J., Dec. 19, 1837. He was educated at Russell's military academy at New Haven, Conn. In the early part of his life he was a farmer, taking charge of the farm at the homestead. After his marriage he moved to his farm at Tinton Falls. He remained there until the fall of 1876, then went to Red Bank, N. J., and spent seven years in mercantile business. A severe illness which caused partial loss of sight obliged him to retire from business, and in the fall of 1890 he moved to Philadelphia, Penn., where his two older sons are in business.

He married, Sept. 16, 1868, HULDA HOLMES VAN MATER, dau. of Gilbert Holmes Van Mater and Sarah Hendrickson Holmes. She was born in Holmdel, Mar. 24, 1844.

CHILDREN.

1. *Robert Gansevoort,* b. Sept. 20, 1869.
2. *Gilbert Van Mater,* b. Nov. 10, 1871.
3. *Henry Gansevoort,* b. Oct. 14, 1875.

---

27. ELIZABETH GANSEVOORT HAZARD, dau. of John V. S. Hazard and Catharine E. Cooke, (16), was born in Albany, N. Y., July 7, 1838, and died in Brooklyn, N. Y., Dec. 14, 1893, aged 55, leaving no children.

She married, Apr. 3, 1879, GERRARD ALLEN, son of Leander Allen and Emmalina Gerrard. He was born in New York City, Dec. 8, 1833, and was an accountant in a bank there for many years. He lives in Brooklyn.

28. MINERVA ELIZABETH ALLEN, dau. of William W. Allen and Helen M. Gansevoort, (21), was born in Bath, N. Y., Dec. 19, 1862.

She married, Oct. 9, 1884, EDWIN STEWART UNDERHILL, son of Anthony Lispenard Underhill and Charlotte Louisa McBeath. He was born in Bath, Oct. 7, 1861. He attended Haverling academy in Bath, and then entered Yale college in 1877, where he graduated in 1881, receiving the degree of A. B. He is editor and publisher of the "Steuben Farmers' Advocate," the oldest paper in the county, and has served many years as chairman of the Democratic county committee. Was Democratic candidate for Presidential Elector in 1888.

CHILDREN.

1. *William Allen,* b. Jan. 28, 1888.
2. *Edwin Stewart, Jr.,* b. Apr. 18, 1890.

GANSEVOORT IRWIN ALLEN, son of William W. Allen and Helen M. Gansevoort, (21), was born in Bath, N. Y., Dec. 1, 1867. He was educated in the Haverling academy in Bath, and at Cornell University. At the latter institution he became a member of the Alpha Delta Phi fraternity, and has since become identified with that club of New York City. Since 1890 he has been engaged in mercantile pursuits and real estate in Steuben county. Is a member of Steuben Lodge, No. 112, F. & A. M., and lives in Bath.

29. ARABELLA STEUART MAGEE, dau. of Duncan S. Magee and Catharine E. Gansevoort, (22), was born in Corning, N. Y., Mar. 23, 1854.

She married, May 12, 1874, ALFRED LEWIS EDWARDS, son of Alfred Edwards and Sophia Matilda Lewis. He was born in New York City, Dec. 2, 1835. He was a graduate of Yale College in

1857, and of Harvard Law School in 1861, and practiced in New York until 1876, then moved to Columbia county, N. Y., and lived near Hudson for several years. He is an elder in the Presbyterian church, and from 1862 to 1874 was a member of the New York Bible Society, holding successively the offices of Corresponding Secretary, Vice President and President. He resides in New York City.

CHILD.

Helen Gansevoort, b. Aug. 10, 1876; m. Archibald K. Mackay. (31)

30. HELEN GANSEVOORT MAGEE, dau. of Duncan S. Magee and Catherine E. Gansevoort, (22), was born in Corning, N. Y., Sept. 5, 1855.

She married, Apr. 19, 1877, LEWIS EDWARDS, son of Alfred Edwards and Sophia Matilda Lewis. He was born on Long Island, N. Y., May 3, 1848. He was educated in the Scientific Department of Columbia College, and is an architect, but has not practiced the profession for several years. He lives in New York City.

CHILDREN.

1. Mary Gansevoort, b. Mar. 17, 1878.
2. Duncan Lewis, b. Oct. 29, 1879.

31. HELEN GANSEVOORT EDWARDS, dau. of Alfred L. Edwards and Arabella S. Magee, (29), was born in Columbia county, N. Y., Aug. 10, 1876.

She married, Nov. 24, 1896, ARCHIBALD KENNEDY MACKAY, son of Barnard Mackay and Mary Christina Auchmuty. He was born in East Hampton, N. Y., Nov. 3, 1866. He graduated at Harvard in 1889, and is a real estate broker in New York City.

BARENT AND JOHN J. ROSEBOOM.

32. BARENT ROSEBOOM, son of John Roseboom and Susannah Veeder, (4), was born in Schenectady, N. Y., June 17, 1771. He sometimes signed himself "Barent J.," to distinguish himself from Capt. Barent, his uncle. His boyhood was passed amid the excitements of the war, which left their impress upon his character in a restless activity which used up life all too fast. About 1790, when he was less than twenty years of age, he with his still younger brothers, John and Abraham, began business as traders on the Mohawk, a mile east of the settlement of Canajoharie, succeeding William Beekman, who had established himself there a couple of years previously as the first merchant in the township after the war. As early as 1776, at or before the organization of Tryon county, a crossing called Martin Van Alstine's ferry had been established at that point. Near this John, the father of the young men, had purchased a farm, and took up his residence upon it to begin life anew after the general break up and scattering of fortunes by the upheaval. The partnership with John continued till 1807.

At about the same time three brothers, traders, John, James and Archibald Kane, put up a stone building with an arched roof, that became well known as the "Round Top." A profitable business was built up in the wheat, potash and other products of the rapidly developing country, and the place became a rendezvous for the adventurous youth of that restless time. Here took place a quarrel in which Barent Roseboom became involved, leading to a duel, according to the false ideas of honor that ruled men in those days. The

encounter took place Apr. 18, 1801, in a pine grove west of the
"Round Top," and Archibald Kane was wounded in the right arm
by Barent's bullet. The affair created a great sensation through
the Valley, and is about the only regretable incident this history
will have occasion to mention, as affecting unfavorably the subjects
of its record in those early days of disturbance.

Barent was a man of enterprise, engaged in numerous ventures
and business connections. His account books from 1796 and
onward show him as partner in a number of firms, first with Philip
Van Alstine, as Van Alstine & Roseboom, established at Canajoharie, in a store on the east side of the creek, the place then consisting of scarce a dozen habitations. At Warren, further up, where
settlement was crowding in so rapidly, was the house of Roseboom,
Van Alstine & Wemple, and at Cherry Valley, now recovering from
the devastation of the massacre, the un-named partner in "John
Diell & Company" was Barent. Here the aged "Uncle Colonel"
Myndert, and later the brothers, John and Abraham, were engaged
in settling or managing lands. Barent lost his wife in 1803, which
broke up his home, but only led to wider plans. The partner at
Warren was called to Canajoharie where a new concern, Van Alstine,
Roseboom & Wemple, continued business on a larger scale, Roseboom to reside at Albany to forward produce, visiting New York
twice a year, as the Articles of co-partnership provided. He con-
tracted a second marriage, with a cousin of his first wife, but died
the next year, in Canajoharie, Mar. 25, 1807, aged 35.

He married, 1st, Apr. 7, 1796, SARAH SCHERMERHORN, dau. of
Simon Jacobse Schermerhorn and Sarah Vrooman. She was born
in Schenectady, Sept., 1775, and died in Canajoharie, Jan. 27,
1803, aged 27.

He married, 2nd, in 1806, CATHARINE TYMS,* dau. of Col.
Johannes Visscher and Susannah Schermerhorn, and widow of
Michael Tyms. She was born in Schenectady, Oct. 20, 1773.
After the death of her husband in 1807, she returned to Schenectady
and resided with his mother and died there, Jan. 21, 1814, aged 40.

---

* Catharine Visscher married, 1st, Michael Tyms, son of Samuel Tyms and Jannetje Van
Pettin. He was born in Schenectady, Sept. 18, 1763, and died there, Aug. 28, 1804, aged 40.

CHILDREN.

1. *Harriet Jane*, b. May 15, 1799; d. Oct. 7, 1800, ae. 1.
2. *Ariaantje Jane*, b. Oct. 30, 1801; d. July 27, 1802.
3. *Samuel John*, b. July 29, 1803; d. Aug. 8, 1804, ae. 1.

CHILDREN:—by the first marriage.

1. *Hendrick Myndert,* b. Oct. 8, 1799; d. June 29, 1824, ae. 24.
2. *Sarah,* b. Aug. 1801; d. Dec. 1, 1801.

HENDRICK MYNDERT ROSEBOOM, son of Barent Roseboom and Sarah Schermerhorn, (32), was born in Canajoharie, N. Y., Oct. 8, 1799. He graduated at Union College, and commenced the study of law in Cherry Valley, in the office of James Brackett, Esq. He fell a victim to consumption and died at the residence of his uncle Abraham, June 29, 1824, aged 24.

JOHN J. ROSEBOOM, son of John Roseboom and Susannah Veeder, (4), was born in Schenectady, N. Y., Oct. 25, 1774. He was in partnership with his brothers in the mercantile business in Canajoharie, N. Y., until the death of his brother Barent, in 1807. Soon after that the home was broken up and with his mother and sister-in-law he returned to Schenectady, and remained until the death of the latter in 1814, when he went to Cherry Valley and resided with his brother Abraham till his death. Ill health prevented his engaging in business after leaving Canajoharie. He died unmarried, Mar. 15, 1829, aged 54.

ABRAHAM ROSEBOOM AND DESCENDANTS

33. ABRAHAM ROSEBOOM, son of Lieut. John Roseboom and Susannah Veeder, (4), was born in Schenectady, N. Y., Aug. 10, 1777. He was associated with his brothers, Barent and John, in the mercantile business in Canajoharie, N. Y., until the death of his father in 1805, when he came to settle upon and improve the lands inherited from his father and uncle, over two thousand acres, in the towns of Cherry Valley and Middlefield. He located in a part of the town, nearly three miles south of the village of Cherry Valley, known from pre-Revolutionary days as the "Beaver Dam Patent," and which is now included in the town of Roseboom, having been set off from Cherry Valley. Mr. Roseboom was opposed to the movement for the division of the township and contested the measure sixteen years, most of that time in the state legislature, then in the board of supervisors, to whom it was afterwards referred. Dr. Alonzo Churchill, then supervisor of the town of Richfield, had the deciding power and agreed to the division, providing the name of "Roseboom" should be given to the new township as a compromise between the two interests. The division was made Nov. 23, 1854.

Mr. Roseboom was an active pioneer and did much to advance the interests of the locality, erecting the first saw-, carding- and fulling mill in the settlement called Lodi, in 1806. On the 19th of June of that year a warrant was granted for the organization of Trinity Lodge, No. 139, F. & A. M., at Cherry Valley; "Dr. Joseph White was its Master for several years, and among the members were Elijah and Lester Holt, and Abraham Roseboom, men of worth and honor." In that same year Mr. Roseboom built the house in which he passed fifty-seven years of married life, and which is still standing, although moved from its original site. On the 24th of Sept., 1856, their Golden Wedding was celebrated by a family gathering Seven children, four children by marriage, and twenty grandchildren, making in all, with the venerable couple, a household of thirty-three, were gathered under the old roof-tree to commemorate this impressive jubilee. The eldest grandchild was just twenty-one years of age, and the youngest a few weeks old. Two sons and one grandchild had died.

Mr. Roseboom was lenient as a landlord and indulgent to the poor. In addition to his landed estate he accumulated quite a fortune by judicious foresight and enterprise. With full faith in the future success of the Albany and Schenectady railroad, and later in the Utica and Schenectady section, both of which were subsequently incorporated in the extensive system of the New York Central R. R., he continued to make investments up to the time of his death. He was for many years a whig in politics, and a warm admirer of Henry Clay, sedulously reading the proceedings of Congress in the "Congressional Globe" every winter. He subsequently became a democrat, but was not a politician and never held office, but was very domestic, simple and regular in his habits and spent a large part of his time in reading. He was noted for uprightness in all matters of business, independence of favors, and punctuality. To owe a debt and not to pay promptly was no better than a theft. He never wasted another's time in waiting. He was regular as the clock in all his movements, so that an invalid girl sitting at her window used daily to remark, "Its now a quarter after eleven, for here comes Mr. Roseboom on his gray horse, on his way home from the village; I can see his white necktie and shirt ruffles." He died at the homestead, Jan. 5, 1867, aged 89.

He married, Sept. 24, 1806, RUTH JOHNSON, dau. of Jesse Johnson and Mary Stevenson, (10). She was born in Chatham, Conn., Mar. 11, 1779. At that time the war of the American Revolution was in progress and her early years were passed amid the many privations incident to those trying times. Very few books were to be had—almost none for children. Nearly all clothing was home-spun, either of flax or wool, cotton sheeting was unknown, and when Mrs. Roseboom began housekeeping her presses were so well stocked from her own spinning that it was many years before new supplies were needed, and some of it is still preserved, little less than a century old. Any account of her would be incomplete without mentioning her constant knitting; usually, with book or paper before her, particularly in the long winter evenings, her needles clicked busily on and steadily grew the stockings and mittens, for her children while they were young, then her grand-children, and later poor children in the city had the benefit of her industry.

She was a faithful and devoted christian, a woman of clear and discriminating views, of strong principles and unbending integrity. She was bountiful in hospitality, and benevolent to self-sacrifice towards every good cause. While her neighbors came confidently to her for help and sympathy, her church and the cause of missions, then in its infancy, received from her hands generous and systematic offerings. She has left to her children a noble example in the grace of giving. She devoted herself to her domestic duties with singular care and fidelity, and still found time to enrich and strengthen her mind with wide and varied reading, and retained much of her mental vigor almost to the last. She died at the homestead, Mar. 2, 1864, aged nearly 85.

CHILDREN.

1. *John,* b. Aug. 10, 1807; d. May 16, 1839, ae. 31.
2. *Susan Maria,* b. July 3, 1809; m. Moses Belcher. (34)
3. *Henry,* b. Aug. 3, 1811; m. Cornelia R. Livingston. (35)
4. *Marietta,* b. Mar. 30, 1813; m. Dr. Joseph White. (36)
5. *Jesse Johnson,* b. Apr. 26, 1815; m. Caroline Cook. (37)
6. *Lucy,* b. Apr. 8, 1817; m. James Shannon. (38)
7. *Elizabeth,* b. Mar. 16, 1819; m. William Hall. (39)
8. *Sarah,* b. Oct. 4, 1822; m. Richard Ely. (40)
9. *Catharine,* b. Apr. 12, 1824; resides in Cherry Valley.

JOHN ROSEBOOM, son of Abraham Roseboom and Ruth Johnson, (33), was born in the town of Cherry Valley, (now Roseboom), N. Y., Aug 10, 1807. He attended the Cherry Valley academy, but when a lad of about fifteen years he went to Albany and was in the store of Isaac and William Staats for some years. In 1832 he entered into partnership with his brother-in-law, Moses Belcher, in Cherry Valley, in the mercantile business and continued in the same until his death. He was Captain of a company of militia for some years and was afterwards promoted to Major. He died unmarried in Cherry Valley, May 16, 1839, aged 31.

34. SUSAN MARIA ROSEBOOM, dau. of Abraham Roseboom and Ruth Johnson, (33), was born in the town of Cherry Valley, (now Roseboom), N. Y., July 3, 1809. She was christened in Schenectady, by the Rev. Mr. Bogardus. Her home for many years joined the grounds of the Cherry Valley Academy, where her children were educated, and in 1873 she moved into the stone mansion on Main street, left unfinished by her son at his death, where she now resides with her daughter and daughter-in-law. Her former home was burned Mar. 29, 1891, and the academy on July 6, 1894.

Retiring and mild in her disposition, full of patient cheerfulness and abounding charity, she has been an example of healthful and lovely old age, failing sight latterly placing some restrictions on her sources of tranquil enjoyment.

She married, Apr. 18, 1832, MOSES BELCHER, son of Elijah Belcher and Elizabeth Putnam. He was born in Cherry Valley, Jan. 1, 1803, of New England parentage, received his education at the academy and then engaged in mercantile pursuits until his death. After his marriage a partnership was formed between his brother-in-law, John Roseboom, and himself, which continued until the death of the latter in 1839. He died in Cherry Valley, Jan. 5, 1841, aged 38.

CHILDREN.

1. *Henry Roseboom*,   b. Mar. 26, 1833; d. Jan. 9, 1835, ae. 1.
2. *Abraham Roseboom*, b. Sept. 28, 1835; m. Elizabeth J. McLean.   (41)
3. *Maria*,   b. July 22, 1837; d. Jan. 10, 1857, ae. 19.
4. *Elizabeth Putnam*, b. Sept. 1, 1839; resides in Cherry Valley.

---

35. HENRY ROSEBOOM, son of Abraham Roseboom and Ruth Johnson, (33), was born in the town of Cherry Valley, (now Roseboom), N. Y., Aug. 3, 1811. He obtained his education at the district school and Cherry Valley academy, and began his business life with two years' service as clerk in the general store of Adolphus W. and Hiram Flint, in Cherry Valley. In 1830 he took a position as clerk in the mercantile house of John R. Pitkin, at 118 Pearl St., New York, that street being at the time the principal avenue for the wholesale business of the city. He boarded in the family of his employer. The firm changed for a time to Pitkin, Boyd & Co., and the location to 11 Hanover St. He remained in New York about four years, in the fall of 1831 making the voyage to New Orleans on his employer's business, and returning by stage,

stopping at Mobile, Washington, and other principal cities, at that ime a notable and most fatiguing trip. During his residence in New York he was one of a large band of young men who fell strongly under the influence of the eminent Dr. Francis L. Hawks, of St. Thomas's church, in Broadway, leading to an interest in the Episcopalian form of religious faith which identified him with that denomination throughout his subsequent life.

In 1834 he formed a business partnership with David Gross, at Fort Plain, N. Y., and during his residence there suffered severely from an attack of acute rheumatism, which yielded only to treatment at the sulphur springs of Sharon, then in a primitive condition. So impressed was he with the curative value of these waters that he framed the project of developing them by the erection of a large hotel at that place, and in 1836 he was instrumental in forming a company, principally of his friends among the merchants of New York, 160 acres of land including the sulphur springs were purchased, and the erection of the Pavilion was begun. In the whirlwind of financial disaster of the succeeding year, 1837, nearly all the members of the company failed, and the property went into chancery. The same storm smote the firm of Gross & Roseboom and it was dissolved in Jan., 1838. Mr. Roseboom subsequently returned to New York and remained there until called to Cherry Valley in 1841, to settle the estate of his brother-in-law, Moses Belcher.

Upon his marriage in 1843 a house was erected for him near his father, who was now advancing in years and needed his assistance in the management of his business. Here he pursued the life of a typical country gentleman, succeeding to the large landed estate on the death of his father in 1867. Like his father he was an indefatigable reader, having a well-stocked library, both of standard works and current literature, and watching the course of events with the closest interest. He was the supervisor of the town of Cherry Valley in 1848, and like his father was opposed to its division. His social and church relations were largely in Cherry Valley, and the project of dividing the town seemed like a sundering of a large part of the natural ties of his family's life.

Mr. Roseboom took a lively interest in agricultural matters and was an active member of the County Agricultural Society, of which he was president for some years. Politically he was a democrat, strongly attached to the principles of that party. Although averse to political distinction he was often called by his fellow citizens to officiate in various offices. He took a leading part in the formation of Grace Church parish and the erection of the edifice; a parish called Trinity had previously existed. Of this he was a communicant and warden from the beginning. A prominent and enterprising citizen, Henry Roseboom enjoyed a recognized position among the more influential men of the county; participated in the councils of his church, and was a trusted friend of the earlier management of the New York Central Railroad Company, in whose enterprise his father had embarked in full faith, from the day when its rude tramway line was first stretched over the ground between Albany and Schenectady, so often traversed by his ancestors in their Indian traffic and subsequent business exchanges. What a space of the career of human progress is embraced between the time when the merchant of Albany made his first tramp to the Indian village of Niscayuna, and the time when his descendant counted the votes as teller of the Central Railroad, with the first Vanderbilt in the chair!

Mr. Roseboom was in New York when the clock was first placed in the tower of the City Hall, May 7, 1831, on which date he wrote, "I can see it from my window, hope it wont wake me too early in the morning;" such was the wonted quietude of the great city in that day, the eternal noises of which now the seven sleepers themselves would find it hardly easy to slumber through unmoved. He divided his landed estate, consisting of about 2,000 acres, between his three sons, portions of the land having been previously sold by his father. He died at the homestead, July 18, 1883, aged nearly 72.

He married, May 24, 1843, CORNELIA RUTGERS LIVINGSTON, dau. of Jacob Livingston and Catharine Augusta De Peyster. She was born in Livingstonville, N. Y., July 9, 1815. Robert Livingston, the first ancestor of the family in America, was born in Ancrum, Scotland, Dec. 13, 1654, and died in Albany, N. Y., Apr. 20, 1725. He was the son of John Livingston, a Scottish Presbyterian divine born in 1603, who was banished in 1663 for non-conformity, and went to Rotterdam, where he died in 1672. Robert emigrated in 1673, settled in Albany, and in 1675 became secretary of the Commissaries, which office he held until Albany became a city in 1686, then was town clerk until 1721. He acquired great influence over the Indians and was secretary of Indian affairs for a long series of years. In 1686 he received from Gov. Dongan the grant of a large tract of land, which in 1715 was confirmed by a royal charter from George I, and is still known as Livingston Manor, though most of the land has passed out of the hands of the family. He married in 1679, Alida, widow of Rev. Nicholas Van Reusselaer, and daughter of Philip Pietersen Schuyler, and had three sons. Philip, the eldest, was second lord of the Manor, born in Albany, July 9, 1686, and died in New York City, Feb. 4, 1749. He was a man of note and influence, holding offices successively till his death. His son, Robert, was the third and last lord of the Manor, and his grandson, Jacob Livingston, of Schoharie and Cherry Valley, was the father of Mrs. Roseboom, and married Catharine Augusta De Peyster. Her first ancestor in America was Johannes De Peyster, who came about 1633. His son, Abraham, was one of the most distinguished men in the province, holding successively the office of Alderman, Mayor, Judge of the Supreme Court, Member of the King's Council as presiding officer, acting Governor in 1700, &c. His son, Abraham, Jr., succeeded his father as treasurer of New York and New Jersey, and held the office forty-six years. (His eldest daughter, Catharine, married John Livingston, of New York.) Col. James De Peyster, son of Abraham, Jr., was the grandfather of Catharine Augusta De Peyster, the mother of Mrs. Roseboom.

Mrs. Cornelia R. Roseboom, with her daughter, Mary, reside at the homestead in the town of Roseboom.

CHILDREN.

1. *Lerantia Livingston,* b. Mar. 31, 1844; m. Rev. Henry C. Swinnerton. (42)
2. *Catharine Augusta,* b. Dec. 30, 1845; d. Aug. 16, 1881, ae. 35.
3. *Mary Eliazbeth,* b. Jan. 9, 1848.
4. *Abraham Hendrick,* b. Feb. 27, 1851; m. Mary D. Ballou. (43)
5. *Jacob Livingston,* b. Apr. 9, 1853; is a physician in Rochester, N. Y.
6. *Ruth,* b. May 31, 1855; m. John Sawyer. (44)
7. *William Campbell,* b. Dec. 25, 1858; d. Jan. 3, 1895, ae. 36.
8. *Cornelia,* b. Aug. 7, 1862; d. Feb. 18, 1863.

---

36. MARIETTA ROSEBOOM, dau. of Abraham Roseboom and Ruth Johnson, (33), was born in the town of Cherry Valley, (now Roseboom), N. Y., Mar. 30, 1813. She is a woman of strong individ-

uality, kind-hearted and generous, and ever ready to give assistance to those in need. Prompted by her love for her Church she erected, in 1873, the stone edifice, the Church of the Good Shepherd, in which Episcopal services have been regularly held, and presented it to the Diocese of Albany as an offering from herself and husband. From the time of her marriage Canajoharie, N. Y., has been her home, and in 1879 she erected the stone dwelling, "Stony Terrace," where she now resides.

She married, Mar. 20, 1845, Dr. JOSEPH WHITE, son of Joseph White and Hannah Gates. He was born in Chatham, Conn., May 9, 1800. He was a direct descendant of Elder John White, who came from England in the ship Lyon, in 1632, and settled in Cambridge, Mass.; was one of the first settlers of Hartford, Conn., in 1636, and of Hadley, Mass., in 1659. In 1805 his parents moved to Middlefield, Otsego Co., N. Y., and engaged in farming, where his early life was spent in hard labor. At the age of twenty-one he left home to begin the study of medicine with his second cousin, Dr. Joseph White, of Cherry Valley, one of the leading physicians in the state. He attended lectures and graduated at the Fairfield Medical College. In 1822 he joined the Cherry Valley Lodge, F. & A. M., and always took great interest in the workings of that Order, and from 1856 to 1872 he was chairman of the Committee on Foreign Correspondence of the Grand Chapter of the state.

In 1824 he went to Penfield, near Rochester, N. Y., and began the practice of his profession. On June 20, 1829, he was appointed Surgeon of the 1st. Regiment of Riflemen of the state, by Lieut. Gov. Enos T. Throop. Ill health obliged him to seek a milder clime and in 1831 he went to Washington, D. C., and opened a drug store near the navy yard. While there he had the cholera in 1832, the first time it appeared in this country, which left him with a disease from which he never fully recovered. In 1835 he bought the drug store of Dr. Theodore Pomeroy, of Cooperstown, N. Y., and continued in business there until Mar. 1, 1838, when he exchanged stores with Philip Roof, of Canajoharie. The next year Seymour N. Marsh, son of Seymour Marsh, the inventor of the Marsh Truss, became a partner and the manufacture of trusses was an important part of their business. White & Marsh sold their drug interests to D. W. Irwin in 1844, but continued the manufacture and sale of trusses until 1849, when they dissolved partnership.

He continued the practice of medicine until the fall of 1878, when increasing ill health compelled him to retire.

His high reputation and fame as a physician and surgeon were not confined to his immediate home but extended throughout the Mohawk Valley and surrounding country, and he was frequently called to distant parts of the state for consultation and to perform difficult operations. He was a most active member of the state and county medical societies. To his zeal and efforts can be attributed many of the enterprises and improvements which aided the advancement and prosperity of the village, notably the academy, water works, Prospect Hill cemetery, and the Cherry Valley and Canajoharie plank road. He was one of the first trustees of the Lutheran church organized in 1839, and it was through his means that St. Polycarp's Episcopal church was established in 1852, the name of which was afterward changed to the Church of the Good Shepherd. Although never free from pain he bore his suffering with great patience and fortitude, and was always cheerful and entertaining, having a fund of anecdote or reminiscence ready to amuse or instruct those who came in contact with him. He died in Canajoharie, Oct. 28, 1884, aged 84.

CHILDREN.

1. *John Roseboom,* b. Mar. 25, 1846; lives in California.
2. *Sarah Elizabeth,* b. Oct. 27, 1848; m. Dr. Peter L. Schenck. (45)
3. *Joseph Henry,* b. Aug. 29, 1855; lives in Canajoharie.

---

37. JESSE JOHNSON ROSEBOOM, son of Abraham Roseboom and Ruth Johnson, (33), was born in the town of Cherry Valley, (now Roseboom), N. Y., Apr. 26, 1815. He remained upon his father's farm until his marriage and then went to Indiana, and settled on a farm about four miles from the present city of La Porte. Himself, wife and both sons were victims of that dread disease, consumption. He died at his home near La Porte, July 7, 1851, aged 36.

He married, Sept. 17, 1845, CAROLINE COOK, dau. of John Cook and Mary Ann Reiley. She was born in Springfield, N. Y., Feb. 16, 1824, and died in Binghamton, N. Y., Mar. 6, 1856, aged 32.

CHILDREN.

1. *John,* b. July 17, 1846; d. Aug. 16, 1870, ae. 24.
2. *Myndert,* b. June 16, 1850; d. Aug. 9, 1875, ae. 25.

38. LUCY ROSEBOOM, dau. of Abraham Roseboom and Ruth Johnson, (33), was born in the town of Cherry Valley, (now Roseboom), N. Y., Apr. 8, 1817. After the death of her husband she returned to her father's and passed her remaining years in Cherry Valley, where she died Feb. 25, 1872, aged 54, leaving no children.

She married, Nov. 22, 1842, JAMES SHANNON, son of Robert Shannon and Anne Kerr. He was born in Ballina, county Mayo, Ireland, Nov. 22, 1811. His father was a prosperous merchant in Ballina, but becoming dissatisfied with the disturbed state of political affairs then existing there, he came to the United States and arrived with his family in Bath, Steuben county, N. Y., in May, 1830. That fall he purchased the Springfield farm, formerly occupied by Col. Charles Williamson, the founder of Bath.

James had received a good education in the old country and soon after his arrival began the study of Law with Hon. William Woods, was admitted to the Bar and opened an office in Bath. He was a lawyer who never practiced the tricks of the trade, and would not espouse the cause of a guilty client. A single incident is characteristic of him: a man applied to him to be defended in a suit, when, from his own admission, he was guilty of a misdeed that was punishable by years of imprisonment. This was his first offense, and instead of defending him, Mr. Shannon read him a serious lecture on his conduct and then, for the sake of a young wife and helpless children, advised him to take leg-bail for Canada, and retrieve the past, which he did and in a short time was able to send for his family and care for them honestly. It was in consideration of the welfare of those innocent ones, on whom the severest weight of his crime would fall, that this unique advice was given, and who shall say he followed not the example of the Master, who once said, "Neither do I condemn thee, go and sin no more?" He died in Bath, June 7, 1848, aged 36.

---

39. ELIZABETH ROSEBOOM, dau. of Abraham Roseboom and Ruth Johnson, (33), was born in the town of Cherry Valley, (now Roseboom), N. Y., Mar. 16, 1819. She was a woman of marked intelligence and vivacity, greatly beloved and admired by the friends she made in her successive places of residence, as well as in the home neighborhood at Cherry Valley, where her children were born and

where her remains were buried by the side of her husband. For about a year after his death she remained in Easton, and then joined her sons in Richmond, Va., where she died suddenly of pneumonia, Feb. 3, 1886, aged 66.

She married, Oct. 6, 1851, WILLIAM HALL, son of Jonathan Hall and Eunice Palmer. He was born in Cherry Valley, Oct. 28, 1818, was educated at the academy and engaged in the mercantile business in that village for some years. In April, 1866, he moved to a farm near Geneva, N. Y., and in 1879 took up his abode in Easton, Penn., where he died Dec. 21, 1884, aged 66.

CHILDREN.

1. *James Shannon,* b. Nov. 2, 1852; m. Josephine Wilson; Cora E. [Le Sueur. (46)
2. *Eunice Maria,* b. Mar. 12, 1855; m. Gansevoort V. V. Cortelyou. (47)
3. *William Edward,* b. Sept. 17, 1859; m. Della Kitchen. (48)

---

40. SARAH ROSEBOOM, dau. of Abraham Roseboom and Ruth Johnson, (33), was born in the town of Cherry Valley, (now Roseboom), N. Y., Oct. 4, 1822. She was educated at the academy, and at the school of Miss Urania Sheldon, (afterwards Mrs. Eliphalet Nott), in Utica, N. Y. She has been a member of the First Presbyterian Church of Binghamton, N. Y., for many years, and has had a large part in its activities. She has also been connected with other philanthropic and religious organizations. Her father said "she was like his mother," greater praise than this, no one need ask; and it may explain the love borne her by all who know her. "In her tongue is the law of kindness," and in every trust she has been found faithful. She has found her greatest happiness in living for others, and this is the reason why in advanced years she has kept her youth. She, with her two surviving daughters, reside in Binghamton.

She married, Sept. 12, 1849, RICHARD ELY, son of Dr. Elihu Ely and Eliza Maria Ely. He was born in Binghamton, Dec. 29, 1819. He was a direct descendant of Richard Ely who came from Plymouth, England, in 1660 and settled in Lyme, Conn. He was of Huguenot descent and a Puritan in the time of Cromwell, and emigrated on the restoration of Charles Second. We next find this family in possession of 4,000 acres of land for which they paid

£300; Richard paying one-sixth of the whole town tax. Some of these lands are still in the possession of the family. Quite a number of this man's descendants became ministers and doctors, and it was proverbial that Lyme was never without a deacon Richard Ely. During the Revolutionary war all the six sons of James Ely, a great grandson of the first Richard, served in the Continental army, one of whom, Elihu, was present at the surrender of Gen. Burgoyne at the battle of Saratoga, Oct. 7, 1777. His sword and powder horn are now in the possession of the family of Richard Ely, in Binghamton. The powder horn has this inscription with Masonic emblems: "For the defense of liberty," "Liberty and no slavery." One William Ely of Lyme, was the first person in that region to free his slaves in 1787. Rev. Richard Ely was born in Lyme, Sept., 1755, and of the third generation from him was Dr. Elihu Ely of Binghamton, who died there in Mar., 1850. He was among the earliest settlers in Broome county about 1812, when Binghamton was called Chenango Point.

Richard, the second son, was sent to Ellington, Conn., where he was fitted for college and graduated from Amherst in 1841. He studied law but gave up the practice to assist in the care of his father when he became a paralytic. In 1849 he was appointed mail agent on the Erie railroad soon after it was opened to travel. In 1854 he opened a forwarding store between the Chenango canal and the Erie railroad, which was burnt in 1867. He then became agent for several insurance companies until his health failed in 1887 and he was a helpless invalid for three years before his death. In 1858 he united with the First Presbyterian church and ever after as far as he was able took up the duties of a christian in his family and in the community. He was genial and social in his nature and had many friends. He died in Binghamton, Apr. 18, 1892, aged 72.

CHILDREN.

1. *Lucy Shannon*, b. Oct. 7, 1850.
2. *Catharine Roseboom*, b. July 19, 1852.
3. *Eliza Maria*, b. Apr. 10, 1854; d. June 13, 1861, ae. 10.
4. *Sarah Roseboom*, b. Aug. 20, 1856; d. Aug. 23, 1883, ae. 27.
5. *Richard Erskine*, b. July 5, 1859; d. Sept. 3, 1860, ae. 1.
6. *Robert Erskine*, b. Sept. 13, 1861; lives in Cambridge, Mass.

CATHARINE ROSEBOOM, dau. of Abraham Roseboom and Ruth Johnson, (33), was born at the homestead, "Beaver Dam Farm," in the town of Cherry Valley, (now Roseboom), N. Y., Apr. 12, 1824. She was educated at the Cherry Valley academy and at the boarding school of Miss Urania Sheldon, (afterward the wife of Dr. Eliphalet Nott), in Utica, N. Y. Upon the death of her father in 1867, she and her sister, Mrs. Shannon, established their home at "West View," in Cherry Valley, where she now resides. Deeply interested in religious undertakings and in education, the present edifice of the Presbyterian church was erected by her in 1872, as a memorial to her parents and sister; and she took part as chief promoter in the resuscitation of the ancient academy in 1881, and gave liberally for its maintenance until it was superseded by the academic department of the Union school in 1895. She has served the missionary cause as treasurer of the Presbyterial society since its organization in 1879. She is Vice-Regent of the Cherry Valley Chapter, Daughters of the American Revolution.

---

41. ABRAHAM ROSEBOOM BELCHER, son of Moses Belcher and Susan M. Roseboom, (34), was born in Cherry Valley, N. Y., Sept. 28, 1835, where he received his academic education and spent his entire life. Although his health precluded his entering upon professional or mercantile pursuits he was a most active and public spirited citizen, and was universally valued for his services and helpfulness. He interested himself in town affairs, was an officer in the Presbyterian church, and carried out the project of enlarging the cemetery in 1867. He died in Cherry Valley, Aug. 10, 1872, aged 36.

He married, Dec. 8, 1868, ELIZABETH JUDD MCLEAN, dau. of Charles McLean and Mary Judd. She was born in Cherry Valley, June 5, 1836, where she now resides.

CHILD.

Mary Louise, b. Sept. 26, 1871; m. Dr. Nathaniel F. Yates. (49)

---

42. LEVANTIA LIVINGSTON ROSEBOOM, dau. of Henry Roseboom and Cornelia R. Livingston, (35), was born in the town of Cherry Valley, now Roseboom,* N. Y., Mar. 31, 1844.

---

* The town of Roseboom was formed from the town of Cherry Valley, November 23, 1854.

She married, June 24, 1871, Rev. HENRY ULYATE SWINNERTON, fourth son of James Swinnerton, of Colnbrook, Middlesex, and Fanny Rutter, of Lymington, Hants, England, who emigrated to America in 1833. He was born in Catskill, N. Y., Oct. 4, 1839. He spent his youth in Newark, N. J., graduated at Princeton with the degree of A. B., in 1863, and attended the Princeton Theological Seminary for three years, receiving the degree of A. M. He preached in Wilmington, Del., in 1866, in Morrisville, Penn., in 1867, and became pastor of the Presbyterian church in Cherry Valley, N. Y., in 1868, where he now lives. In 1877 the degree of Ph.D. was conferred upon him by Union College. He has written constantly for the secular as well as the religious press, and in 1876 published a "Historical Account of the Presbyterian Church of Cherry Valley."

CHILDREN.

1. *John Roseboom*,   b. Apr. 30, 1872; d. May 1, 1872.
2. *Cornelia Livingston*, b. Dec. 12, 1873.
3. *Catharine Roseboom*, b. July 19, 1876.
4. *Sylvia Agnes*,   b. Oct. 9, 1878.
5. *Susan Elizabeth*,   b. Nov. 15, 1880.
6. *Rosamond Rutter*,   b. Mar. 22, 1883.

---

43. ABRAHAM HENDRICK ROSEBOOM, son of Henry Roseboom and Cornelia R. Livingston, (35), was born in the town of Cherry Valley, now Roseboom, N. Y., Feb. 27, 1851. He was educated in the Cherry Valley academy, Deer Hill Institute, Danbury, Conn., and Cornell University. He was for a time civil engineer on the Canada Southern R. R., and then went to Red Wing, Minn. He took a claim of Government land in Renville county, and was a farmer until 1889, when he went to Hutchison, Minn., and was assistant cashier in the Citizens' bank till 1896, when he retired to "Rosemary Farm," near Lakeside, Minn.

He married, Sept. 27, 1876, MARY DEXTER BALLOU, dau. of Hosea Ballou and Sarah Sprague Vaughan. She was born in New Orleans, La., Feb. 3, 1851. She is a direct descendant of Rev. Hosea Ballou, who was born in Richmond, N. H., Apr. 30, 1771, and died in Boston, Mass, June 7, 1852. He was one of the founders of American Universalism, and pastor of the Second Universalist Society in Boston from 1817 to 1852.

CHILDREN.

1. *Hendrick,* b. Aug. 7, 1877.
2. *Catharine Augusta,* b. Oct. 6, 1881.

Dr. JACOB LIVINGSTON ROSEBOOM, son of Henry Roseboom and Cornelia R. Livingston, (35), was born in the town of Cherry Valley, now Roseboom, N. Y., Apr. 9, 1853. He was fitted for college by Rev. Josiah Clark, at Northampton, Mass., and entered Yale in the fall of 1872, graduating with the degree of A. B., in June, 1876. He then entered the office of David Little, M. D., of Rochester, N. Y., as a student of medicine, took a course in chemistry at the University, and in Mar., 1878, became senior assistant in the City hospital.

He attended lectures at the College of Physicians and Surgeons, New York City, during the winters of 1876-80 and received the degree of M. D. from that institution in Mar., 1880. In Nov. of that year he was appointed assistant physician at the Kings County hospital, Flatbush, L. I., and filled that position until July, 1881, when an attack of typhus fever compelled his resignation. From 1882 to '84 he practiced in Utica, N. Y., and was appointed a ward physician, a visiting physician to the Utica Orphan Asylum, was a member and librarian of the Utica Medical Library Association, a member of the Medical Society of Oneida County, and of the Oneida Historical Society.

The year 1885 was spent in study at Marburg, Germany, and at the University of Vienna, and in travel. He returned in July, 1886, and in Dec. of that year settled in Rochester. The following spring he was appointed one of the City physicians and held that office three years. He is U. S. Examiner for Pensions, fellow and councillor of the Rochester Academy of Sciences, and member of the following organizations: Rochester Pathological Society; Medical Society of Monroe County; Staff of the City hospital; Rochester Lodge, No. 660, F. & A. M.; Ionic Chapter, No. 210, R. A. M.; Cyrene Commandery, No. 39, K. T.

44. RUTH ROSEBOOM, dau. of Henry Roseboom and Cornelia R. Livingston, (35), was born in the town of Roseboom, May 31, 1855.

She married, Oct. 2, 1883, JOHN SAWYER, son of John Labaree Sawyer and Charlotte Root. He was born in Delhi, N. Y., Nov. 20, 1861. Two years later his parents moved to Cherry Valley, N. Y. He graduated at Union College in 1881, with the degree of A. B. For several years he was connected with various New York papers as special correspondent, and then became associated with his father in publishing the "Cherry Valley Gazette," until the death of the latter, Mar. 9, 1897, when he assumed entire charge of the paper. He was supervisor of the town in 1891–2.

CHILDREN.

1. *Blanche Labaree,* b. July 20, 1884.
2. *John LeRoy,* b. Dec. 3, 1885.
3. *Henry Roseboom,* b. Dec. 6, 1889.
4. *Irving Rutgers,* b. Aug. 17, 1894.

WILLIAM CAMPBELL ROSEBOOM, son of Henry Roseboom and Cornelia R. Livingston, (35), was born in the town of Roseboom, N. Y., Dec. 25, 1858. He was the namesake of his uncle by marriage, Judge William W. Campbell. After attending various boarding schools he entered Union College in 1878 and graduated in 1882. He travelled extensively throughout this country, as far as California and Florida, visited the exposition at New Orleans in 1885, and at Chicago in 1893. In 1889 he was one of a bicycle party to visit Europe, attending the exposition at Paris; and in 1891 he went to the Bermuda Isles with a similar party. In 1890 he became a member of the Monroe Cigar Co., Rochester, N. Y., and continued in that business until his death at Cherry Valley, N. Y., Jan. 3, 1895, aged 36.

JOHN ROSEBOOM WHITE, son of Dr. Joseph White and Marietta Roseboom, (36), was born in Canajoharie, N. Y., Mar. 25, 1846. He attended the academy in that place, Gilmore's school in Ballston Spa, and Eastman's Business College in Poughkeepsie, graduating June 28, 1864. In the fall of that year he entered the employ of the N. Y. Central railroad company at Albany, in the General

Passenger Accountant's office, became Gen'l Pass. Acc't in 1867, and filled that position until Dec., 1871, when the offices were moved to New York. July 3, 1866, he joined the Albany Burgesses Corps, the second oldest independent military company in the state, being organized in 1833; he won the Wendell drill and discipline medal in 1869, was recording secretary in 1870–1, and was made a life member in 1874.

In the spring of 1872 he went to the Pacific Coast and in Oct., accepted a position with Graves, Maynard & Co., bankers and brokers, in Gold Hill, Nev., until they retired from business in July, 1873, when he entered the employ of the bankers, D. Driscoll & Co., in Virginia City, Nev. The summer of 1876 was spent east, visiting his home and the Centennial Exposition at Philadelphia, and he resumed his position in Sept. In the spring of 1877 he became connected with the Virginia City agency of the Nevada Bank of San Francisco, until Oct., 1879, when he was made local secretary of the Virginia and Gold Hill Water Company, was also appointed local secretary the next year of the Sierra Nevada Wood and Lumber Company, and later was elected secretary of the Nevada Mill and Mining Company, remaining connected with those corporations until Apr., 1885, when he returned to his early home in Canajoharie.

In the spring of 1886 he entered into partnership with A. W. Ehle, in the Granite, Marble and Monumental business in that place, which was continued three years. He organized and was captain of the Drill Corps of the Protection Engine and Hose Company. In Nov., 1893, he returned to the Pacific Coast, and from May, 1894 to Dec., 1895, was in the employ of Gen. S. H. Marlette, in Carson City, Nev. He lives in California.

---

45. SARAH ELIZABETH WHITE, dau. of Dr. Joseph White and Marietta Roseboom, (36), was born in Canajoharie, N. Y., Oct. 27, 1848.

She married, June 10, 1896, Dr. PETER LAWRENCE SCHENCK, son of John Schenck and Catharine Van Dyke Ryder. He was born in Flatbush, (now Brooklyn), N. Y., Oct. 25, 1843. He is a lineal descendent of Johannes Schenk, who emigrated from Middleburg, Holland, to this country in 1683. The family is traced back in

Holland through a long descent to the time of Charlemagne.

His early education was received at Erasmus Hall academy, Flatbush, where he was prepared for the sophomore class of the University of the City of New York, from which institution he graduated in 1862, receiving three years later the degree of A. M. After graduation he entered the College of Physicians and Surgeons, New York, which conferred on him the degree of Doctor of Medicine in 1865. He served one year as assistant physician in the King's County hospital, and entered his country's service as acting assistant surgeon, U. S. A., and was several months in charge of a hospital at Wilmington, N. C., terminating his services at the close of the war.

In 1866 he was assistant physician in the cholera hospital at South Brooklyn, residing there from its opening until its close. He was then appointed assistant resident physician at the Kings County hospital, which position he occupied until 1872, when he was appointed to take charge of the hospital as medical superintendent. He served in that capacity until 1881, when he resigned to engage in private practice in the City of Brooklyn, which occupation he has since followed.

He is a member of the Kings County Medical Society, American Academy of Medicine, Brooklyn Pathological Society, and is examining surgeon to Midwood Council of the National Provident Union, and consulting surgeon to the Kings County hospital. He was for some years surgeon to the Brooklyn Jockey Club, and attending physician in the Kings County penitentiary. He has been a member of the Crescent, Montauk, Zeta Psi, and Carleton clubs, being president of the latter for two terms. As a member of the Masonic fraternity he has been Master of Montauk Lodge for two years, and District Deputy Grand Master for the third district of New York, for 1887-8. He has written two works, both genealogical,— "Memoir of Johannes Schenk, of Bushwick, Long Island," and a "Historical Sketch of the Zabriskie Homestead,"— both of which were privately printed.

JOSEPH HENRY WHITE, son of Dr. Joseph White and Marietta Roseboom, (36), was born in Canajoharie, N. Y., Aug. 29, 1855. He received his education in the schools of that village and Palatine

Bridge. In 1873 he purchased an amateur printing outfit and during 1876-7 published an amateur monthly, "The Lilliputian." He was corresponding secretary of the New York State Amateur Press Association, for 1877, and attended the meeting of the National Amateur Press Association, at Long Branch, N. J., in July, of that year. In 1878 he was a partner of J. A. Miller, as job printers, in Canajoharie, but disposed of his interest to Mr. Miller the next year.

In the fall of 1883 he went to California *via* the Isthmus of Panama, being thirty-five days on the trip, and returned east in May, 1885. In Nov., 1886, he again visited California, and the next year became interested in the fancy poultry business at "Woodside" ranch, in the Sycamore Valley, with his cousins, under the firm name of White & Wood. That year he joined Danville Grange, No. 85, Patrons of Husbandry, and still retains his membership. He has attended two meetings of the National Grange; at Concord, N. H., in 1892, and at Syracuse, N. Y., in 1893.

In May, 1890, he returned to his eastern home. Ill health in early youth has prevented his taking part in the more active occupations of life, and the severe winters are passed in milder climes; those of 1882 and 1886 were spent in the Bermuda Isles, 1891 in Florida, and the subsequent ones in Washington, D. C. For many years he has been interested in Philately, and is a member of several philatelic societies. Genealogy has occupied his attention for the past two years, assisting in the preparation of this volume. He lives with his mother, in Canajoharie.

---

46. JAMES SHANNON HALL, son of William Hall and Elizabeth Roseboom, (39), was born in Cherry Valley, N. Y., Nov. 2, 1852. In May, 1873, he went to Faribault, Minn., and engaged in general farming and nursery business. In Aug., 1877, he moved to Waseca, Minn., where he was a druggist until Mar., 1884, when he joined his parents in Easton, Penn. The next spring he went to Richmond, Va., where he now lives and is engaged in the real estate business.

He married, 1st, Jan. 6, 1874, JOSEPHINE WILSON, dau. of Samuel Wilson and Eliza Rutherford. She was born in Geneva, N. Y.,

Mar. 7, 1850, and died in Faribault, Mar. 31, 1876, aged 26, leaving no children.

He married, 2nd., June 14, 1893, CORA ETTA LE SUEUR, dau. of Little Berry Le Sueur and Henrietta Lightfoot. She was born in Buckingham county, Va., Mar. 1, 1869.

---

47. EUNICE MARIA HALL, dau. of William Hall and Elizabeth Roseboom, (39), was born in Cherry Valley, N. Y., Mar. 12, 1855.

She married, Sept. 15, 1892, GANSEVOORT VAN VRANKEN CORTELYOU, son of Gerrit Cortelyou and Katherine Jane Brinckerhoff. He was born in Hackensack, N. J., Jan. 15, 1854. He graduated at Rutgers College in 1875, and then studied ecclesiastical decoration and commercial designing and practiced the same until 1884, and is now engaged in the grain exporting trade. He lives in Elizabeth, N. J.

CHILD.

Pierre Van Wyck, b. Dec. 16, 1895.

---

48. WILLIAM EDWARD HALL, son of William Hall and Elizabeth Roseboom, (39), was born in Cherry Valley, N. Y., Sept. 17, 1859. In 1883 he became a junior partner in a shirt manufacturing company in Easton, Penn., until 1885 when he joined his brother in the purchase of a farm near Richmond, Va. In June, 1892, he went to Buckingham county, Va., where he is a member of the White-Hall Lumber Co., which has founded and built the prosperous and growing young town of White Hall.

He married, Mar. 9, 1891, DELLA KITCHEN, dau. of William Penn Kitchen and Elizabeth Coffin Osterstock. She was born in Easton, Mar. 14, 1860.

CHILD.

Emily Elizabeth, b. Nov. 26, 1891.

Rev. ROBERT ERSKINE ELY, son of Richard Ely and Sarah Roseboom, (40), was born in Binghamton, N. Y., Sept. 13, 1861. After receiving his preparatory education at the high school there, from which he graduated with the highest honors, being the valedictorian of his class, he entered Amherst College, completing his course in 1885. He was one of the first ten men in scholarship rank in his college class and therefore the distinction was conferred upon him of election in the first "drawing" to membership in the Phi Beta Kappa Society. He entered Union Theological Seminary in New York City, in the autumn of 1885, completing the course in 1888, when he was one of the four men chosen to represent his class by a public part at the commencement exercises.

Licensed to preach by the Manhattan Congregational Association of New York City, in May, 1888, he began his ministry on June 1st, as pastor of Stearns Chapel, in Cambridge, Mass., a mission connected with the Prospect street church. In Dec., 1890, the mission became Hope church, and he was ordained minister. Nov. 1st, 1892, he resigned his charge in order that he might devote more time to the evening school and college for the benefit of working men, in Cambridge, in connection with Harvard University, known as The Prospect Union. This institution was founded by Mr. Ely, with the aid of Prof. Francis G. Peabody, of Harvard, and other persons, in Jan., 1891. He was chosen to be the first president of the Union and continues to hold that office. He is also president of the Co-operative Union of America, and of the Co-operative Printing Society of Cambridge; and pastor of the Union Parish Church of Arlington Heights. His chosen lifework is to uplift and help laboring men, giving right direction to their energies and some brightness to their lot.

---

49. MARY LOUISE BELCHER, dau. of Abraham R. Belcher and Elizabeth J. McLean, (41), was born in Cherry Valley, N. Y., Sept. 26, 1871, and died there, July 8, 1895, aged 23.

She married, July 12, 1894, DR. NATHANIEL FERDINAND YATES, son of Trevor Yates and Martha Moore. He was born in the town of New Lisbon, N. Y., July 8, 1858. His grandfather, Dr. William Yates, was born in England, in 1767. He attended the first course of lectures ever delivered by Dr. Abernethy. To more than ordinary talents was added great benevolence. He established a private insane asylum where the patients were treated on the humane plan. He came to America in 1799, previous to which he had become greatly interested in vaccination, just becoming known to the medical profession in England. He made the acquaintance of Dr.

Jenner and obtained from him a large supply of virus, and immediately on his arrival in Philadelphia he engaged with the zeal of an ardent and philanthropic mind to disseminate the knowledge of the new discovery. It is certain that he was the first to introduce into America this great boon to humanity, although the credit of this introduction has been generally accorded to another. He purchased a large estate in what is now the town of Morris, Otsego Co., N. Y., married a young lady in the Butternuts Valley, and passed the remainder of his life in that home.

Dr. N. F. Yates was educated in the district school at Noblesville, at the Fairfield Seminary, and the Delaware Literary Institute at Franklin. He was seven years in a drug store, two years in the medical department of the University of Michigan, and graduated at the Long Island College Hospital in 1892, commencing active practice in Cherry Valley, where he now lives.

CHILD.

Florence Mary, b. June 10, 1895.

ROBERT JOHNSON AND DESCENDANTS.

50. ROBERT JOHNSON, eldest son of Jesse Johnson and Mary Stevenson, (10), was born in Chatham, Conn., Aug. 9, 1769. A handsome and promising young man, he chose to follow the sea, a vocation quite common among the young men of the Connecticut valley. He was captain of a sailing vessel plying between New England, New York and southern ports, notably the West Indies. On a homeward voyage in the spring of 1799 his vessel with several others encountered a terrific storm and were lost with all on board, not one survived to bring any certain news, and months of trying suspense followed, but no tidings ever came. He was in his 30th year.

He married, Sept. 9, 1798, LUCY WILCOX,* dau. of Ozias Wilcox and Mabel Gould. She was born in Middletown, Conn., Aug. 22, 1774, and died in Little Falls, N. Y.

CHILD.

Maria Mabel, b. Jan. 27, 1800: m. Rev. Washington Thacher. (51)

---

51. MARIA MABEL JOHNSON, dau. of Robert Johnson and Lucy Wilcox, (50), was born in Middletown, Conn., Jan. 27, 1800, and died in Onondaga, N. Y., July 30, 1827, aged 27.

---

* Mrs. Johnson married, 2nd, Sept. 30, 1808, Dr. James Kennedy. (See foot-note to Family 105.)

She married, July 17, 1822, Rev. WASHINGTON THACHER,* son of Dea. Moses Thacher and Sally Read. He was born in Attleborough, Mass., Feb. 23, 1794. He was descended from a long line of ministers; according to the family tradition sixteen successive generations furnished each their full quota of clergymen to the Christian Church in England and this country. He was a lineal descendent of Rev. Thomas Thacher, the first pastor of the Old South Church, in Boston. His father, a son of Rev. Peter Thacher, of Attleborough, was one of a colony from that place, about the commencement of this century, to found a new settlement at Harford, Penn. Here Washington Thacher entered the select school of Rev. Lyman Richardson, and later his classical school, where his fondness for study soon gave him the prestige of a good English and classical scholar.

He studied theology under the Rev. John Truair, of Cherry Valley, N. Y., and in 1821 was licensed to preach by the Presbytery of Otsego, and was ordained, probably, at Morrisville, N. Y., where he served as stated supply until 1826. He then settled as pastor of the Presbyterian church of Onondaga Valley, remaining there until 1833, when he accepted a call to the first Presbyterian church of Jordan, N. Y., and was installed by the Presbytery of Cayuga. After a long and successful pastorate failing health compelled him to resign. Improving in health he became the principal of Jordan academy, and a year later went to Eaton, N. Y., where he served the church as stated supply for three years.

In July, 1847, he was appointed corresponding secretary of the Central Agency, at Utica, N. Y., of the American Home Missionary Society, which post he filled with decided ability, until by over-exertion and exposure a protracted illness hastened the end. In 1825 he received the degree of A. M. from Hamilton College, and for many years he was a trustee of the Auburn Theological Semi-

---

* Rev. Washington Thacher married, 2nd, Dec. 17, 1828, Sarah Eells Morrell, who was born in New York City, July 10, 1802, and died in Utica, Feb. 27, 1849, aged 46.

CHILDREN.

1. *George Washington*, b. July 19, 1831; m. Sept. 1, 1870, Alice Nautilla Lewis;
   d. Apr. 6, 1895, ae. 63.
2. *Edward Morrell*, b. July 7, 1833; d. June 10, 1855, ae. 21.
3. *Elizabeth Ann*, b. July 2, 1835; m. Sept. 6, 1859, Philip N. Schuyler;
   d. May 5, 1865, ae. 29.
4. *William Whitlock*, b. Jan. 2, 1837; m. Oct. 6, 1880, Marion Louisa Barnum.

nary. He was a thorough scholar and able writer, and in all the relations of life, public and private, the happiness and good of others were his chief consideration. He died in Utica, June 29, 1850, aged 56.

CHILDREN.

1. *Lucy Maria*,	b. June 25, 1823;	m. Dr. Linus P. Brockett.		(52)
2. *Robert Johnson*,	b. May 25, 1825;	m. Martha S. Southwick.		(53)
3. *Sarah Malvina*,	b. July 20, 1827;	m. Orlo R. Damon.		(54)

52. LUCY MARIA THACHER, dau. of Rev. Washington Thacher and Maria M. Johnson, (51), was born in Morrisville, N. Y., June 25, 1823. She resides in Brooklyn, N. Y.

She married, Dec. 22, 1846, Dr. LINUS PIERPONT BROCKETT, son of Rev. Pierpont Brockett and Sarah Sage. He was born in Canton, Conn., Oct. 16, 1820. His early education was obtained at the Conn. Literary Institution, and at Brown University, R. I. He studied medicine in Washington, D. C., and attended lectures at the College of Physicians and Surgeons in New York, graduated from the Yale Medical College, Feb., 1843. Soon after entering upon the practice of his profession his health became seriously impaired, and as a change of climate seemed desirable, he went to Georgetown, Ky., where he practiced some and lectured in Georgetown College.

In the winter of 1845-6 he returned to the east with somewhat improved health, but still so uncertain that he abandoned his profession and after a brief period in the book business, entered upon his life work as an author. He contributed largely to Magazines, Reviews and Periodicals; many elaborate articles from his pen appearing in "Barnard's Journal of Education." His philanthropic tastes led him to feel a deep interest in the care and training of the dependent classes, making thorough investigation into the condition of the blind, the deaf-mutes, the insane and the idiotic. In 1854 he was a commissioner to prepare a report on the condition and history of Idiocy in the state of Conn., and his report is to this day one of the standard documents in the literature of Idiotic instruction.

In 1855 he accepted a position on the editorial staff of the New American Cyclopedia, and later was connected with Johnson's Cyclopedia, and others; his articles being geographical, biographical historical, educational, theological and medical. In 1857 Amherst College conferred on him the honorary degree of A. M. Meanwhile the Civil War came on and his previous training fitted him to enter with great zeal into the literature called forth by the war. He wrote a number of campaign lives of generals and admirals, and aided in several histories of the war. Subsequently he wrote "Woman's Work in the Civil War," costing him an immense amount of labor, and having a very large circulation. He was the author of "Our Western Empire," "The Crescent and the Cross," "Philanthropic Results of the War," "The Early Protestants of the East," and many other volumes.

In 1888 he began to contribute to the "Missionary Review of the World." He wrote well, accumulating his material by patient investigation, and his scholarly attainments and kindly heart rendered him always helpful to the many who sought information. His nature was genial and lovable, and he was particularly helpful to young men who were struggling for an education. He died in Brooklyn, Jan. 13, 1893, aged 72.

CHILD.

Arthur Thacher, b. Oct. 6, 1847; d. Jan. 31, 1854, ae. 6.

53. ROBERT JOHNSON THACHER, son of Rev. Washington Thacher and Maria M. Johnson. (51), was born in Morrisville, N. Y., May 25, 1825. He was educated at the Jordan academy, and then went to Waterville and became a clerk in Mr. Bacon's store. Later he engaged in the hat and cap business in Hamilton, and in 1847 moved to a farm near Marshall, where he lived for ten years, when he became a partner of J. L. Salisbury, Waterville, in the mercantile business. In 1870 ill health compelled him to retire from active life and in 1873 he moved to Rome, N. Y., where he died Jan. 13, 1890, aged 64.

He married, Dec. 16, 1846, MARTHA SOPHIA SOUTHWICK, dau. of Benjamin Southwick and Clarissa Barton. She was born in Sangerfield, N. Y., June 22, 1826, and resides in Rome.

CHILDREN.

1. *Benjamin Washington,*	b.	Dec. 19, 1847;	d. Sept. 13, 1897, ae. 49.	
2. *Clara Maria,*	b.	July 28, 1849;	m. Albert B. Keeney.	(55)
3. *Caroline Ida,*	b.	Sept. 29, 1850;	m. Ploudon R. Huggins.	(56)
4. *Mary,*	b.	Dec. 8, 1863;	m. Frank H. Carroll.	(57)

54. SARAH MALVINA THACHER, dau. of Rev. Washington Thacher and Maria M. Johnson, (51), was born in Onondaga, N. Y., July 20, 1827. She resides in Detroit, Mich.

She married, Oct. 19, 1853, ORLO ROCKWELL DAMON, son of Rufus Damon and Abigail Andrews. He was born in Bridgewater, N. Y., Apr. 29, 1821, and died in Waterville, N. Y., Aug. 19, 1872, aged 51.

CHILDREN.

1. *Susan Augusta,* b. Mar. 10, 1856; d. Mar. 27, 1857, ae. 1.
2. *George Thacher,* b. Mar. 13, 1858; m. Nellie Mead. (58)

BENJAMIN WASHINGTON THACHER, son of Robert J. Thacher and Martha S. Southwick, (53), was born in Sangerfield Center, N. Y., Dec. 19, 1847. He was educated in Waterville, and was then employed in a store in that place for two or three years. In Sept., 1871, he entered the treasurer's office of the New York, Oswego & Midland Railroad, at Norwich, N. Y., and in 1873 the road became the New York, Ontario & Western, and the office was moved to New York, where he served until Mar., 1881, as clerk, cashier, general clerk, and general passenger and freight agent. That year he went to Laredo, Texas, and became cashier and auditor of the northern division of the Mexican Railroad, then being built from that point to Mexico. Upon the completion of the road in the fall of 1888, his headquarters were transferred to Mexico City, and he became general auditor. In Oct., 1889, he was appointed general passenger and freight agent, which position he held in that city, until his death, Sept. 13, 1897, aged 49. His remains were brought to Rome, N. Y., for interment.

55. CLARA MARIA THACHER, dau. of Robert J. Thacher and Martha S. Southwick, (53), was born in Sangerfield Center, N. Y., July 28, 1849, and died in Rome, N. Y., Mar. 10, 1884, aged 34.

She married, Sept. 15, 1875, ALBERT BARNES KEENEY, son of Rufus Keeney and Sarah Ann Matteson. He was born in Beloit, Wis., Jan. 19, 1846. When he was less then a year old his parents moved to Rome, where he lived until his death. He was educated in the high school there, and at the age of twenty-one he became associated with his father in the hat, cap and fur business, but retired from the firm a short time before his death, Apr. 11, 1884, at the age of 38.

CHILDREN.

1. *Florence Matteson,* b. June 19, 1876.
2. *Lilian Thacher,* b. Jan. 3, 1879.
3. *Clarence Rufus,* b. May 8, 1882.

56. CAROLINE IDA THACHER, dau. of Robert J. Thacher and Martha S. Southwick, (53), was born in Marshall, N. Y., Sept. 29, 1850.

She married, Nov. 16, 1870, PLOUDEN REUBEN HUGGINS, son of Ploudon Huggins and Maria Harrington. He was born in Waterville, N. Y., July 4, 1843. While young his parents moved to Belleville, N. Y., where he was educated in the Union Academy. Then the family returned to Waterville, and in Aug., 1863, he enlisted for four years in the U. S. Marine Corp and took part in several land engagements in addition to the off-shore service. He was on the "Mohican" at the bombardment of Fort Fisher and the first assault which resulted in its capture. In Feb., 1865, he secured an honorable discharge and entered the employ of Candee & Son, general merchants of Waterville, where he remained until 1870, when he bought a farm in Des Moines county, Iowa, and lived in that state for eleven years, being part of the time in the mercantile business in Morning Sun. In 1881, he moved to Rome, N. Y., where he is engaged in the insurance and real estate business.

CHILDREN.

1. *Martha Maria,* b. Nov. 8, 1871.
2. *Thacher,* b. July 24, 1873; d. Aug. 8, 1878, ae. 5.
3. *Albert,* b. Sept. 9, 1876.
4. *Roscoe,* b. Mar. 9, 1880.
5. *Mary,* b. Jan. 16, 1883.

57. MARY THACHER, dau. of Robert J. Thacher and Martha S. Southwick, (53), was born in Waterville, N. Y., Dec. 8, 1863.

She married, Jan. 19, 1886, FRANK HINCKLEY CARROLL, son of Kiron Carroll and Frances Hinckley. He was born in Rome, N. Y., Nov. 8, 1859. Was educated at the Rome academy, graduated in

1876, studied law with his father and was admitted to the Bar in 1881. The next year he went to Michigan, and lives in Pontiac, of which city he was elected mayor in 1895, and again in '96. He is auditor of the Pontiac, Oxford and Northern Railroad. As a member of the Masonic fraternity he is a Pastmaster of Pontiac Lodge, and Captain General of Pontiac Commandery, Knights Templar.

---

58. GEORGE THACHER DAMON, son of Orlo R. Damon and Sarah M. Thacher, (54), was born in Waterville, N. Y., Mar. 13, 1858.

He married, June 12, 1883, NELLIE MEAD, dau. of Fabius Junius Mead and Eleanor MacConnell. She was born in Kankakee, Ill., Oct. 31, 1865. She resides in Chicago, Ill.

CHILDREN.

1. George Mead, b. Oct. 4, 1884.
2. Fabius Junius Ferdinand, b. Dec. 14, 1886.

ELIZABETH JOHNSON STEWART AND DESCENDANTS.

59. ELIZABETH JOHNSON, dau. of Jesse Johnson and Mary Stevenson, (10), was born in Chatham, Conn., June 18, 1773. In 1819 she moved with her children to the town of Cherry Valley, N. Y., and settled on a farm adjoining that of her father. In 1835 she with her daughter, Abigail, went to La Porte, Ind., taking a packet boat on the canal at Fort Plain for Buffalo, a trip of five days, hence by Lake Erie to Detroit where her son Samuel met them, and the drive to La Porte took eight days. She made her home with her sons until her death, Sept. 10, 1851, aged 78.

She married, Apr. 9, 1794, SAMUEL STEWART, son of Daniel Stewart and Elizabeth Stewart. He was born in Chatham, Aug. 14, 1772, and was a farmer. He died there, Apr. 27, 1817, aged 44.

CHILDREN.
1. *Daniel,* b. Oct. 22, 1796; m. Eliza Ensign. (60)
2. *Eliza,* b. Oct. 2, 1798; m. Dr. Eleazer Aspinwall; William [Wilson. (61)
3. *Robert Johnson,* b. Jan. 20, 1801; d. June 30, 1801.
4. *Samuel, Jr.,* b. May 10, 1804; m. Phebe Norton. (62)
5. *George William,* b. Aug. 27, 1807; d. 1835, ae. 28.
6. *Abigail Johnson,* b. Dec. 22, 1813; d. June 13, 1851, ae. 37.

60. DANIEL STEWART, son of Samuel Stewart and Elizabeth Johnson, (59), was born in Granville, Mass., Oct. 22, 1796. He moved to Cherry Valley, N. Y., in 1819, and subsequently engaged in the milling business in Fly Creek, and later in the southern part of the town of Cherry Valley. In June, 1836, he left with his wife and sons for the west, driving to Buffalo with their household goods

in a lumber wagon. There they took a steamer for Detroit on June 16, and were four days and nights on the lake, owing to rough weather. The roads were extremely bad in Michigan, and the best horse died when they were one hundred miles from La Porte, Ind., which was reached on July 6. He resumed milling for some time and then settled on a farm where he died July 26, 1875, aged 78.

He married, Mar. 15, 1827, ELIZA ENSIGN, dau. of Perris Ensign. She was born Jan. 26, 1805, and died in La Porte, Mar. 10, 1849, aged 44.

CHILDREN.

1. *George William,* b. Feb. 8, 1828; d. Dec. 9, 1877, ae. 49.
2. *Harvey Porter,* b. Nov. 17, 1829; d. June 20, 1851, ae. 21.
3. *Henry Roseboom,* b. Sept. 5, 1835; m. Maria E. Rhinehart. (63)
4. *Helen Maria,* } b. Sept. 5, 1838; resides in La Porte.
5. *Sarah Elizabeth,* } b. Twins. d. Nov. 24, 1852, ae. 14.
6. *Harriet Abigail,* b. Sept. 28, 1841; m. Nelson S. Brand. (64)
7. *Lucy Johnson,* b. Dec. 14, 1844; m. Dr. George Merritt. (65)

---

61. ELIZA STEWART, dau. of Samuel Stewart and Elizabeth Johnson, (59), was born in Chatham, Conn., Oct. 2, 1798, and died in La Porte, Ind., Aug. 29, 1847, aged 48, leaving no children.

She married, 1st, Dr. ELEAZAR ASPINWALL, who died in Terre Haute, Ind., between Sept. 20, and Nov. 24, 1820.

She married, 2nd, Feb. 16, 1843, WILLIAM M. WILSON,* son of

---

* W. M. Wilson married, 1st, Eliza Gard, dau. of Rev. Stephen Gard and Mary Pierce. She was born near Trenton, Ohio, Aug. 16, 1802, and died in La Porte county, May 23, 1835, aged 32.

CHILDREN.

1. *Squire,* b. 1826; d. 1828.
2. *Stephen Gard,* b. Sept. 21, 1828; m. Aug. 22, 1848, Sarah Jane Matthews.
3. *Nancy Ann,* b. July 25, 1833; m. Dr. Philander Loomis;
 d. Sept. 26, 1869, ae. 36.
4. *John McClintock,* b. 1835; d. 1835.

He married, 2nd, May 19, 1836, Anna Pierce, dau. of Squire Pierce and Nancy Gray. She was born in Butler county, Ohio, Dec. 23, 1813, and died in Clinton Township, Ind., Jan. 25 1842, aged 28.

CHILDREN.

5. *Margarette,* b. Feb. 25, 1837.
6. *Mary,* b. Sept. 21, 1838; m. Apr. 26, 1857, Sylvester Taber.
7. *John McClintock,* b. May 20, 1840; m. Dec. 25, 1859, Maria Golden.

He married, 4th, Oct. 5, 1848, Permelia Johnson, dau. of David and Mary Johnson, and widow of Christopher C. Johnson. She was born near Lynchburgh, Va., Oct. 17, 1807, and died in La Porte, Mar. 22, 1856, aged 48.

He married, 5th, Mar. 17, 1859, Mary Dinwiddie, dau. of Francis Windle and Eleanor Holt, and widow of David Dinwiddie. She was born in Chester county, Penn., Mar. 3, 1799, and died n La Porte, Dec. 26, 1882, aged 83.

James Wilson and Nancy McClintock. He was born in Northumberland, Penn., Mar. 17, 1791, and was a farmer. He died in Clinton township, Ind., Dec. 22, 1861, aged 70.

---

62. SAMUEL STEWART, Jr., son of Samuel Stewart and Elizabeth Johnson, (59), was born in Chatham, Conn., May 10, 1804. In 1819 the family moved to Cherry Valley, N. Y., and settled on a farm. He was captain of a military company there and his sword is still in the family. In the spring of 1834 he started with his sister Eliza for the west in a covered wagon, and after a long tedious journey they settled on a farm about three miles from the present city of La Porte, Ind. There were but few houses where now stands that beautiful city; all lumber, dry goods, groceries, &c., had to be purchased at Michigan City, fifteen miles distant. He was a staunch Episcopalian and one of the founders of the church in La Porte. He was justice of the peace for two terms in Pleasant township, and a member of the legislature in 1846. He died in La Porte, Jan. 18, 1849, aged 44.

He married, Mar. 7, 1838, PHEBE NORTON, dau. of Dr. Stephen Norton and Sarah G. Hollister. She was born in New Lebanon, N. Y., Aug. 9, 1814, and resides in La Porte.

CHILDREN.

1. *John Roseboom*, b. Dec. 11, 1839; m. Mary M. Sheldon; Ellen P. Smith. (66)
2. *Marietta*, b. Apr. 3, 1842; m. DeWitt C. McCollum. (67)
3. *Sarah Elizabeth*, b. Nov. 6, 1844; d. Feb. 11, 1858, ae. 13.
4. *Robert Samuel*, b. Aug. 24, 1848; m. Eliza E. Mossholder. (68)

---

63. HENRY ROSEBOOM STEWART, son of Daniel Stewart and Eliza Ensign, (60), was born in the town of Cherry Valley, N. Y., about four miles south of the village of that name, Sept. 5, 1835. The next year his parents moved to Indiana, and his early life was spent on a farm in La Porte county. Arriving at manhood he went to Plymouth, Ind., and was an engineer on the Wabash railroad for about twelve years, when he settled on a farm two and one-half miles west of Plymouth, where he died Apr. 18, 1883, aged 47.

He married, Dec. 24, 1865, MARIA ELIZA RHINEHART, dau. of

Abraham Rhinehart and Cevica Moore. She was born in Plymouth, July 11, 1846, where she now resides.

CHILDREN.

1. *George Porter,* b. Oct. 19, 1866; m. Celeste Rayder. (69)
2. *Lucy Etta,* b. Nov. 27, 1874; m. William BonDurant. (70)
3. *Coral Helen,* b. July 38, 1878.

---

64. HARRIET ABIGAIL STEWART, dau. of Daniel Stewart and Eliza Ensign, (60), was born in La Porte, Ind., Sept. 28, 1841. She resides in Olathe, Kans.

She married, Mar. 2, 1864, NELSON SAMUEL BRAND, son of Allen Brand and Eliza Downer Lathrop. He was born in Conesville, N. Y., May 29, 1836. He was a descendant of Benjamin Brand, a British officer and sea captain, who brought his family to America about 1744, and settled in Conn. Nelson was a farmer and mechanic, and in the spring of 1857 went to La Porte. In the fall of 1861 he enlisted in Company C, 48th Reg., Indiana Volunteer Infantry, and served until Feb. 14, 1862, when he was discharged for disabilities. He then lived in numerous places and engaged in various occupations until July, 1888, when he went to Kansas City, Mo., where he died Jan. 2, 1896, aged 59.

CHILDREN.

1. *A daughter,* b. May 22, 1870; d. June 7, 1870.
2. *Allen Stewart,* b. Mar. 30, 1872; is a mechanic and lives in Olathe.

---

65. LUCY JOHNSON STEWART, dau. of Daniel Stewart and Eliza Ensign, (60), was born in La Porte, Ind., Dec. 14, 1844, and died in Pittsburg, Penn., Jan. 18, 1887, aged 42, leaving no children. She was interred at the Cherry Valley, N. Y., cemetery.

She married, June 25, 1878, Dr. GEORGE MERRITT,* son of

---

* Dr. Merritt married, 1st, June 18, 1851, Fannie Cornelia Gilbert, dau. of Rev. Sturges Gilbert and Martha Cheney White. She was born in Great Barrington, Mass., Dec 29, 1829, and died in Cherry Valley, May 19, 1877, aged 47.

CHILDREN.

1. *Fannie Amelia,* b. Apr. 8, 1852; m. Oct. 12, 1874, Samuel Alfred McClung.
2. *George Little,* b. Apr. 6, 1853; m. July 31, 1882, Carrie Adah Hillman.
3. *Julia Augusta,* b. July 5, 1855; m. June 18, 1891, Charles Willis Bronson.
4. *Martha Isabel,* b. Mar. 22, 1857.
5. *Ida,* b. Apr. 2, 1860; d. Apr. 20, 1860.
6. *Jennie,* b. Sept. 10, 1861; d. Nov. 25, 1861.
7. *Edith Gilbert,* b. Mar. 24, 1865; m. Apr. 15, 1891, Harry Stanley Giles.

Joseph Merritt and Charlotte Smith. He was born in Cherry Valley, Feb. 9, 1829. He began the study of medicine in the office of Dr. Menzo White, in the latter part of 1845, continuing there three years, then attended the spring term of lectures at the Geneva, N. Y., Medical College and the fall term of the Medical College at Castleton, where he graduated. This last is now the medical department of the University of Vermont. He commenced the practice of his profession in Cherry Valley in 1850, and continued therein until his sudden death. He was for several years Supervisor of the town, and was an active Mason for forty-five years. His only son, George L., succeeds him in an extensive practice. He died in Cherry Valley, Oct. 26, 1895, aged 66.

66. JOHN ROSEBOOM STEWART, son of Samuel Stewart, Jr., and Phebe Norton, (62), was born in La Porte, Ind., Dec. 11, 1839. He was a farmer in that county until 1878, when he went to Nebraska, and lived in Omaha, Fort Calhoun, Waterloo and Schuyler, being in the latter place seven years. He followed various branches of business as opportunity afforded. In 1889, he went to Lewis county, Washington, and has a fruit ranch near Newaukum.

He married, 1st, Mar. 28, 1860, MARY MARIA SHELDON, dau. of Correl Charles Sheldon and Eliza Humphrey. She was born in Olean, N. Y., Apr. 29, 1842, and died in La Porte, Feb. 25, 1871, aged 28.

He married, 2nd, Nov. 26, 1872, ELLEN PAULINA SMITH, dau. of John Derlin Smith and Harriet Eliza Austin. She was born in La Porte, Dec. 9, 1851.

CHILDREN ;— by the first marriage.

1. *Eliabeth*, b. Mar. 18, 1861; m. Frank A. Churchill. (71)
2. *Henrietta*, b. Mar. 1, 1868; m. John H. Long. (72)

CHILDREN ;— by the second marriage.

3. *Jessie Delina*, b. Oct. 19, 1873.
4. *Marietta*, b. Feb. 24, 1887.
5. *Frances*, b. July 29, 1889.

67. MARIETTA STEWART, dau. of Samuel Stewart, Jr., and Phebe Norton, (62), was born in La Porte, Ind., Apr. 3, 1842.

She married, Sept. 11, 1866, DeWitt Clinton McCollum, son of George Sherwood McCollum and Achsa Wing. He was born in La Porte, May 10, 1842. He was a farmer until Aug. 11, 1862, when he enlisted as 2nd Sergeant in Company 1, 87th Regiment, Indiana Volunteers, but served in the capacity of Orderly Sergeant. His regiment was first engaged at the battle of Perryville, Ky., Oct. 8, 1862, and participated in all the skirmishes and marches through Ky. and Tenn., up to the battle of Chickamauga where it was again engaged on the 19th and 20th days of Sept., 1863. For meritorious conduct in this battle he was recommended by his colonel and commissioner as First Lieut. of his company, Jan. 21, 1864, and on the first day of Apr., he took command of his company until the close of the war on account of the Captain being absent on detached service.

His regiment participated in all of the battles in front of Atlanta, Ga., including that of Jonesboro, and entered the city with the balance of the army. He was in the great campaign with Sherman to the sea, or to Savannah, and was with the army through the Carolinas to Raleigh, where Joseph E. Johnston surrendered the Confederate army to Sherman; after which marched north to Richmond, and to Washington, and was in the grand review. Was honorably discharged as Brevet Captain on June 14, 1865, by reason of the close of the war.

He returned to farm life but after three years commenced mercantile business in La Porte. He was one of the Board of Commissioners appointed by Gov. Gray and the State officers of Indiana that built the Soldiers' and Sailors' monument at Indianapolis, which cost $400,000. In the winter of 1895-6 he joined the soldiers' colony at Fitzgerald, Ga., until 1897. He lives in La Porte.

CHILDREN.

1. *Georgiana*,   b. Oct. 31, 1867: d. Apr. 12, 1871, ae. 3.
2. *Samuel Stewart*,   b. June 5, 1870.
3. *George Sherwood*, b. Jan. 6, 1874.
4. *Edwin John*,   b. Apr. 9, 1879.
5. *Eraline*,   b. Jan. 21, 1882.

---

68. ROBERT SAMUEL STEWART, son of Samuel Stewart, Jr., and Phebe Norton, (62), was born in La Porte, Ind., Aug. 24, 1848.

In Sept., 1887, he went to Wellington, Kansas, where he was employed by Wells, Fargo & Co. In the spring of 1893 he went to Kansas City, Mo., and is in the employ of the city railroad company.

He married, Dec. 31, 1879, ELIZA ETTA MOSSHOLDER, dau. of Richard Mossholder and Christena Fredrica Hilt. She was born in Minerva, Ohio, Apr. 18, 1848. She resides in La Porte.

CHILDREN.

1. *Cora Ada*, b. Jan. 8, 1882.
2. *Edith Rowena*, b. July 9, 1886.

---

69. GEORGE PORTER STEWART, son of Henry R. Stewart and Maria E. Rhinehart, (63), was born in Plymouth, Ind., Oct. 19, 1866. He was educated in the public school, learned telegraphy in 1886, and was then employed by the Penn. R. R. Company, and in 1893 became train dispatcher at Fort Wayne, Ind.

He married, June 20, 1893, CELESTE RAYDER, dau. of Jesse Finley Rayder and Nellie Keating. She was born in Plymouth, July 13, 1871.

CHILD.

Zillah Marguerite, b. Oct. 19, 1894.

---

70. LUCY ETTA STEWART, dau. of Henry R. Stewart and Maria E. Rhinehart, (63), was born in Plymouth, Ind., Nov. 27, 1874.

She married, Oct. 27, 1896, WILLIAM BONDURANT, son of Jeptha BonDurant and Mary Elizabeth Balsley. He was born in Plymouth, Dec. 23, 1868. He is a professional artist, and lives in South Bend, Ind.

---

71. ELIZABETH STEWART, dau. of John R. Stewart and Mary M. Sheldon, (66), was born in La Porte county, Ind., Mar. 18, 1861.

She married, Sept. 26, 1877, FRANK ALBERT CHURCHILL, son of Franklin George Churchill and Amelia Laman. He was born in Addison, N. Y., Dec. 7, 1856. He lives in Bradford, Penn., and is editor-in-chief of "The Bradford Evening Star."

CHILD.

Helen, b. Sept. 13, 1879.

72. Henrietta Stewart, dau. of John R. Stewart and Mary M. Sheldon, (66), was born in La Porte, Ind., Mar. 1, 1868.

She married, Mar. 1, 1893, John Henry Long,* son of William Henry Long and Socelia Wirick. He was born in Columbus, Ohio, Nov. 27, 1845. He left for Iowa in 1860, and three years later went to Boise City, Idaho, and the following year to Lewis county, Washington. On this long journey he drove an ox team to pay for his board. He is a man of natural ability and had good educational advantages, and was soon recognized as a leader in the pioneer community in which he lived. In 1868 he was elected Assessor of Lewis county, and two years later County Treasurer. He was Representative in 1876, Territorial Councilman in 1880, and State Senator in 1889. He was spoken of for Governor in 1892, but owing to the death of his son Charles, he refused the nomination. He lives near Chehalis, and is a farmer.

CHILD.

Letitia, b. Jan. 4, 1894.

---

* J. H. Long married, 1st, Mar. 5, 1868, Deborah Waterman Hodgdon, dau. of Stephen Hodgdon and Deborah Bosworth. She was born in Halifax, Mass., Mar. 6, 1850, and died in El Paso, Tex., Feb. 7, 1892, aged 41.

CHILDREN.

1. *Florence Adelaide*, b. Dec. 3, 1868; m. Sept. 5, 1888, William Burton Allen.
2. *Charles Elmer*, b. May 22, 1871; d. July 10, 1892, ae. 21.
3. *Frederick William*, b. Sept. 7, 1873.
4. *Stanley Bosworth*, b. Nov. 2, 1875.
5. *Oscar Stephen*, b. Apr. 3, 1880; d. Jan. 1, 1881.
6. *Josephine Mabel*, b. June 28, 1881.
7. *Harry Waterman*, b. July 12, 1885.

MARY JOHNSON WILDER AND DESCENDANTS.

73. MARY JOHNSON, dau. of Jesse Johnson and Mary Stevenson, (10), was born in East Haddam, Conn., May 17, 1775. She was an intelligent, well-balanced, affectionate, christian woman, unselfishly devoted to her family and domestic duties. In 1837 she and her daughter Lucy went to Claridon, Ohio, and after the latter's marriage she made her home with her son, Eli, in Painesville, Ohio, where she died, Sept. 10, 1849, aged 74.

She married, Oct. 23, 1796, Col. ELI WILDER, son of Dea. John Wilder and Hannah Austin. He was born in Hartland, Conn., May 2, 1770. From a book of the Wilder Family, published in 1878, by Rev. Moses H. Wilder, of Brooklyn, N. Y., the following is gleaned: "The first Wilder of whom we have knowledge was Nicholas, a military chieftain in the army of the Earl of Richmond, at the battle of Bosworth Field, Aug. 22, 1485. On Apr. 15, 1497, being the twelfth year of the reign of Henry VII, the latter gave to Nicholas as a token of his favor a landed estate with a coat of arms, which estate is still held by his heirs.

Thomas, of the fourth generation from Nicholas, died in 1634, leaving a widow Martha and five children, John, Thomas, Elizabeth, Edward and Mary, all of whom in 1638 emigrated to Massachusetts Bay. Thomas settled in Charlestown, was made a freeman in 1640 and died in 1692. From him in direct line came John, a farmer of Lancaster, Mass., born in 1646; John, also a farmer of Lancaster, bap. Mar. 12, 1673; Jonas, born in Lancaster, in 1699, moved to Lyme, Conn., in 1733, and to Hartland in 1760, where he died in 1797. The "Connecticut Historical Collections" has the following notice of the latter, taken from the "Hartford Courant," of 1796, by a Hartland correspondent: "There is now living in this town a Mr. Jonas Wilder, in the 97th year of his age, a steady, industrious man, seldom losing a day's work by reason of infirmity or old age. He is the oldest man in the town by several years. He has had two wives, both of the same name, both christian and maiden; with the last he has lived over sixty years. He has had thirteen children, all of whom are living, the oldest being 73, and the youngest 46 years of age. His sons, seven in number, have sustained the following honorable offices besides town and society offices: one colonel, one major, one captain, two lieutenants, three justices of the peace, three representatives and three deacons. His posterity were numbered in 1795, and found to be 232, all but 15 of them were then living." His son, Dea. John, was the father of Col. Eli, and died in 1805.

Col. Eli Wilder was a gentleman of the old school, courteous and gracious in his manners, refined in his speech, and enjoyed the confidence of his town's people to a remarkable degree, being elected magistrate for many years. He was colonel of the militia of his district and served several terms in the legislature. Though constitutionally conservative he was a man of broad and tolerant spirit. He died in Hartland, Aug. 14, 1835, aged 65.

CHILDREN.

1.	*Calvin,*	b.	May 9, 1798;	m.	Phebe Wilder.	(74)
2.	*Mary Louisa,*	b.	Aug. 7, 1800;	m.	Lester Taylor.	(75)
3.	*Horace,*	b.	Aug. 20, 1802;	m.	Phebe J. Coleman.	(76)
4.	*Lucy,*	b.	Dec. 10, 1804;	m.	Dr. Erastus Goodwin.	(77)
5.	*Robert Johnson,*	b.	Jan. 16, 1807;	d.	Oct. 27, 1826, ae. 19.	
6.	*John Andrews,*	b.	Feb. 12, 1809;	d.	Aug. 11, 1827, ae. 18.	
7.	*Hannah,*	b.	Apr. 12, 1811;	d.	July 7, 1813, ae. 2.	
8.	*Eli Trumbull,*	b.	Nov. 13, 1813;	m.	Julia W. Wakefield; Larissa M. [Kendig.	(78)
9.	*Seth Loomis,*	b.	May 28, 1816;	m.	Harriet Thayer; Lydia B. [Grout.	(79)
10.	*A daughter,*	b.	Sept. 9, 1818;	d.	Sept. 21, 1818.	
11.	*Hannah Elizabeth,*	b.	Jan. 26, 1823;	d.	Dec. 3, 1825, ae. 2.	

74. CALVIN WILDER, son of Col. Eli Wilder, and Mary Johnson, (73), was born in Hartland, Conn., May 9, 1798. He was a farmer and lived on the old homestead with his father. In 1823 he held the office of town clerk. For some time he carried the mail between Hartland and Hartford, and was one of a military company known in those days as "Troopers." He died suddenly in Winsted, Conn., Sept. 13, 1832, aged 34.

He married, Dec. 26, 1821, PHEBE WILDER, dau. of Thomas Wilder and Tryphena Austin. She was born in Barkhamsted, Conn., Sept. 9, 1799, and died in Jefferson, N. Y., Feb. 14, 1874, aged 74.

CHILDREN.

1. *Mary Louisa*, b. May 12, 1823; m. Watson E. French. (80)
2. *Austin Joseph*, b. Sept. 9, 1824; m. Marinda Pickett; Mary H. Thomas. (81)
3. *Deloss Dwight*, b. Feb. 23, 1826; m. Maranda F. Finch. (82)
4. *Lucy Ann*, b. Apr. 15, 1828; d. Sept. 4, 1846, ae. 18.
5. *Susan*, b. Aug. 20, 1830; m. Watson E. French. (83)

75. MARY LOUISA WILDER, dau. of Col. Eli Wilder and Mary Johnson, (73), was born in Hartland, Conn., Aug. 7, 1800, and died in Claridon, Ohio, May 5, 1870, aged 69.

She married, May 2, 1821, Lester Taylor, son of Childs Taylor and Rhoda Bates. He was born in Hartland, Aug. 5, 1798. Soon after their marriage they started for their new home, a log house in the woods, in Claridon, Ohio, and were four weeks on the road with a pair of horses and wagon. He had been there previously and taught school in the winter, in Mentor, in a log house. His ninety scholars were from eleven different states, with as many different school books. They lived in their log house seven years, till it was burned with nearly everything in it. He was Colonel of the militia in 1828, and Associate Judge under the old state constitution. In 1830, the Ohio legislature chose him one of three commissioners to survey, appraise and sell sixty thousand acres *of land for the Western Reserve School fund. He was sent to the legislature as Representative in 1832 and '34, and again in 1844–5; and to the Senate in 1856–7. Was elected Speaker *pro tem* of the Senate and served most of the time during the two sessions, as the Lieutenant

Governor was absent much of the time. He called the Senate to order the first time they met in the new State House. He was Justice of the Peace in 1845 and Associate Judge of the Court of Common Pleas from 1847 to 1850.

In 1882, fifty years after he was a member of the House first, he was invited to Columbus as ex-member, and on his entrance to each branch the rules were suspended and he was publicly introduced from the Speaker's stand and made a speech. Ten years later he again visited Columbus when the same courtesies were shown him. He was the member of the Congregational church connected with the association of Congregational churches of Lake and Geauga counties, and was the presiding officer for fifteen years from its organization, and was three times sent as delegate to the National Councils; to the first Council in Boston in 1865, to Detroit in 1877 and to Minneapolis in 1895.

He was for many years president of the first Agricultural Society of the county, and is now the only living Charter member. He was the first president and still remains so of the Pioneer Society, and never failed to be present at their meetings till 1895, but was able to preside as usual the next year. For years he was a favorite speaker at Pioneer meetings in other counties as well as his own, often addressing thousands in the woods from the stump, in the city opera houses and public halls. He delivered a Fourth-of-July oration in 1820, and on July 3, 1897, after speaking for forty minutes at the Burton celebration in the forenoon, he went to Claridon and spoke for over half an hour in the afternoon, seventy-seven years later.

Making no claim to be a prophet or the son of a prophet, in introducing public speakers he three times named them as future Presidents; at a convention in Chardon he introduced Mr. Hayes as the next Governor and future President of the United States; Gen. Garfield was introduced by him at Chardon as the next Representative in Congress and future President, and at Burton in 1894 he introduced Mr. McKinley as the candidate for Governor and the next Republican President, which he lived to see fulfilled.

He did not have a liberal education, only attending school winters till he was sixteen, and teaching several winters in Conn. and Ohio. The farm where he first settled is still his home and he intends to pass the remaining days of his life under the time-honored roof.

CHILDREN.

1. *Robert De Witt,*   b. June 19, 1824;   d. Mar. 1, 1830, ae. 5; killed by the [fall of a tree.
2. *La Royal,*   b. May 27, 1827;   m. Anna B. Cleveland.   (84)
3. *Mary Johnson,*   b. Apr. 1, 1830;   resides in Claridon, Ohio.
4. *Lester De Witt,*   b. Dec. 1, 1832;   m. Carmelia Brainard.   (85)
5. *Lucy Wilder,*   b. Aug. 19, 1835;   m. Clinton Goodwin.   (86)
6. *Jane Sophia,*   b. Nov. 23, 1837;   m. William D. Ringland.   (87)
7. *Susan Roseboom,*   b. Apr. 16, 1841;   m. Ozro R. Newcomb.   (88)

---

76. HORACE WILDER, son of Col. Eli Wilder and Mary Johnson, (73), was born in Hartland, Conn., Aug. 20, 1802. He graduated at Yale College in 1823, studied law while a private tutor in Virginia and was there admitted to practice. In 1827 he went to Ashtabula, Ohio, and continued the practice of his profession there till 1836, when he went to Conneaut, Ohio, but returned to Ashtabula in the winter of 1862–63. Ranking with the ablest members of the Ohio Bar, he was elected Judge of the Common Pleas and District Courts of the Ashtabula district, and in 1863 he became one of the Judges of the Supreme Court of Ohio. He was colleague at the Bar with R. P. Ranney, B. F. Wade and J. R. Giddings. His legal integrity is illustrated by an incident of stormy times: at a convention for nominating judge, it was proposed to pledge the nominee not to remand a fugitive slave back to his master, notwithstanding the U. S. Supreme Court had declared the law to be constitutional. Horace Wilder refused to pledge himself as to what his holding might be in any case before hearing it, agreeing with Lord Mansfield on a similar occasion, "that if a man gives a right sentence upon hearing one side only, he is a wicked judge, because he is right by chance only and has neglected taking the proper method to be informed."

In May, 1867, he retired from practice and went to Red Wing, Minn., where he resided with his brother Eli. The relations of these brothers was of rare and delicate amity. In an address before the council of the Episcopal Church, Bishop Whipple said of him: "Hon. Horace Wilder, of Christ Christ, Red Wing, was one who lived by the Prophet's rule,— ' to do justly, to love mercy, and to walk humbly with God. I never looked into his gentle face without thinking that in him, the hoary head was a crown of glory, for he was found in the way of Righteousness.'"

One of the oldest graduates of Yale College, he had won the highest honors in his profession, but his highest honor was that like Nathaniel of old:—"he was a man in whom there was no guile." He died in Red Wing, Dec. 26, 1889, aged 87.

He married, Oct. 29, 1833, PHEBE JERUSHA COLEMAN, dau. of Dr. Elijah Coleman and Phebe Spencer. She was born in Ashtabula, Mar. 27, 1815, and died in Conneaut, Aug. 18, 1847, aged 32.

CHILDREN.

1. *Edgar Seddon,* b. June 16, 1838.
2. *Arthur Morson,* b. Dec. 16, 1840; lives in Red Wing.
3. *Alice,* b. Apr. 30, 1843; d. Dec. 8, 1844, ae. 1.
4. *Horace Coleman,* b. July 3, 1845; d. Mar. 1, 1846.
5. *Julia,* b. July 29, 1847; d. Feb. 8, 1848.

77. LUCY WILDER, dau. of Col. Eli Wilder and Mary Johnson, (73), was born in Hartland, Conn., Dec. 10, 1804, and died in Burton, Ohio, Sept. 25, 1878, aged 73, leaving no children.

She married, Feb. 28, 1848, DR. ERASTUS GOODWIN,* son of Michael Goodwin and Elizabeth Smith. He was born in New Hartford, Conn., Feb. 3, 1784. He studied medicine with his brother-in-law, Dr. Thomas C. Brinsmade, moved to Ohio in 1811, and settled in Burton. He was one of the earliest physicians in that section and had an extensive practice; a skillful practitioner and a man much respected by the community. He died in Burton, Jan. 1, 1869, aged 84.

---

* Dr. Goodwin married, 1st, Feb. 20, 1814, Dotia Gilbert, dau. of Judge Gilbert. She was born in Weybridge, Vt., in 1791, and died in Burton, Nov. 11, 1846, aged 55.

CHILDREN.

1. *Sherman Gould,* b. Nov. 21, 1811; m. Apr. 15, 1838, Lydia Cook;
   d. Jan. 8, 1884, ae. 69.
2. *Erastus Lloyd,* b. July 17, 1818; m. June 9, 1853, Laura Peet;
   d. Jan. 6, 1884, ae. 65.
3. *Homer Michael,* b. Oct. 15, 1819; m. Oct. 29, 1840, Maryette Cowles;
   d. July 6, 1896, ae. 76.
4. *Mary Eliza,* b. Dec. 7, 1822; m. Oct. 8, 1849, Dr. Eden Porter Peters;
   d. June 6, 1875, ae. 52.
5. *Margaret Maria,* b. Apr. 28, 1832; m. Apr. 19, 1852, Edward Sharpe Ross.
6. *Lewis Hunt,* b. Dec. 29, 1833; m. Jan. 23, 1858, Harriet Elvira Smith.

78. ELI TRUMBULL WILDER, son of Col. Eli Wilder and Mary Johnson, (73), was born in Hartland, Conn., Nov. 27, 1813. He left there in Feb., 1833, for Ashtabula, Ohio, and entered the office of his brother Horace, and in Aug., 1835, was admitted to the Bar. He returned to Conn., where he remained two years and then went to Painesville, Ohio, and commenced professional life as a member of the firm of Hitchcock & Wilder. In the spring of 1854, he was appointed a Judge of the Court of Common Pleas, and of the District Court, by the Governor of Ohio, to fill a vacancy. A newspaper clipping says of him, in a notice of his brother Horace: " Who, acquainted with the Bar of Ashtabula, Lake and Geauga counties twenty years ago, does not remember them as among the foremost, and in some respects the foremost, of its able members?"

In 1856 he moved to Red Wing, Minn., where he now resides. " For over thirty years Eli T. Wilder has been an honored and most respected citizen of Red Wing, esteemed and beloved by her people for his public and private charities, and justly prominent in the state as a jurist, and one of the most active and influential of the lay members of the Episcopal Diocese."

He married, 1st, May 22, 1839, JULIA WRIGHT WAKEFIELD, dau. of Dr. Luman Wakefield and Betsy Rockwell. She was born in Winsted, Conn., Oct. 1, 1815, and died in Red Wing, Feb. 16, 1866, aged 50.

He married, 2nd, Oct. 1, 1868, LARISSA MATILDA KENDIG, dau. of Daniel S. Kendig and Maria Southwick. She was born in Waterloo, N. Y., Jan. 30, 1826.

CHILDREN:— by the first marriage.
1. *Ann Wakefield*, b. May 18, 1841; d. May 6, 1848, ae. nearly 7.
2. *Eliza Seymour*, b. Sept. 6, 1846; d. Mar. 24, 1851, ae. 4.
By adoption, *Ella Roeck*.*

79. SETH LOOMIS WILDER, son of Col. Eli Wilder and Mary Johnson, (73), was born in Hartland, Conn., May 28, 1816. He located in Winsted, Conn., and was a partner of Dea. John Hinsdale in mercantile business, and also in the employ of Rockwell &

---

* Ella R. Wilder was born in Hammondsport, N. Y., Oct. 8, 1855. She married, Dec. 19, 1877, Henry Arthur Willard, son of Swante John Willard and Anna Matson. He was born in Red Wing, Feb. 10, 1856.

Hinsdale, a well-known firm of fifty years ago. At the time of his death he was manager of the Thayer Scythe Works. He died in Winsted, Sept. 27, 1864, aged 48, leaving no children.

He married, 1st, Sept. 10, 1840, HARRIET THAYER, dau. of Wheelock Thayer and Clarissa Fuller. She was born in Winsted, July 22, 1822, and died there, June 23, 1857, aged 34.

He married, 2nd, Apr. 10, 1858, LYDIA PIERCE GROUT,* dau. of Rufus Barton and Nancy Goddard, and Widow of Edwin Grout. She was born in Millbury, Mass., Mar. 23, 1813, and died in Worcester, Mass., Feb. 2, 1895, aged 81.

---

80. MARY LOUISA WILDER, dau. of Calvin Wilder and Phebe Wilder, (74), was born in Hartland, Conn., May 12, 1823, and died in Winsted, Conn., Nov. 26, 1846, aged 23.

She married, Aug. 28, 1843, WATSON EMERSON FRENCH, son of Rufus Hewitt French and Clarissa Tiffany. He was born in Hartland, Dec. 7, 1821, and was a mechanic. For forty years he lived about two and one-half miles north-east of Riverton, Conn., where he died June 3, 1893, aged 71.

CHILDREN.

1. *Calvin Wilder,* b. Aug. 23, 1844; d. Aug. 19, 1860, ae. nearly 16.
2. *Mary Louisa,* b. Sept. 2, 1846; m. George H. Ramsbotham. (89)

---

81. AUSTIN JOSEPH WILDER, son of Calvin Wilder and Phebe Wilder, (74), was born in Hartland, Conn., Sept. 9, 1824. When a young man he went to Jefferson, N. Y., and followed the trade of carpenter during all his life. He was of an earnest christian character and respected by all who knew him. He died in Jefferson, Sept. 25, 1878, aged 54.

He married, 1st, Aug. 27, 1856, MARINDA PICKETT, dau. of Jeremiah Pickett and Sophia Ruland. She was born in Jefferson, Oct. 10, 1825, and died there, Apr. 8, 1868, aged 42.

---

* Lydia P. Barton married, 1st, Dec. 1, 1836, Edwin Grout, son of Jonathan Grout and Sally De Wolf. He was born in Millbury, Aug. 4, 1812, and died in Boston, Mass., May 26, 1846, aged 33.

CHILD.

Lydia Ann, b. Dec. 1, 1844; m. Sept. 18, 1866, Arthur Augustus Goodell; Sept. 4, 1883, Col. Fred Williams Wellington.

He married, 2nd, Mar. 16, 1870, MARY HAVENS THOMAS, dau. of Orrin Thomas and Betsey Elizabeth Rose. She was born in Jefferson, Feb. 18, 1841, and lives near Stamford, N. Y.

CHILD: — by the first marriage.
1. *Orville Howd*, b. June 3, 1857; m. Carrie F. Merrill. (90)

CHILDREN: — by the second marriage.
2. *Robert Forest*, b. Aug. 6, 1871; is a farmer in Jefferson.
3. *Phebe Elizabeth*, b. Feb. 3, 1874; m. Frank Hoagland. (91)
4. *Deloss*, b. Feb. 6, 1876; d. Mar. 4, 1876.
5. *Ella Thomas*, b. Nov. 10, 1877.

---

82. DELOSS DWIGHT WILDER, son of Calvin Wilder and Phebe Wilder, (74), was born in West Hartland, Conn., Feb. 23, 1826. After years of hard labor on the farm, he went to California in 1853, taking seven months to complete the journey overland. He worked in the Placer county mines with varied success until June, 1859, when he started a small dairy in Marin county with a capital of $200. This proved successful and in 1871 he moved to Santa Cruz, and entered into an extensive business in the same line with L. K. Baldwin, the partnership continuing until 1885, when it was dissolved by mutual consent. The property then consisted of 4,030 acres, with two ranch houses two miles apart. Mr. Wilder purchased the lower portion containing 2,330 acres for $32,000 in addition to his original one-half interest in the entire property. Situated four miles north of Santa Cruz, natural advantages and yankee ingenuity have made "Wilder's Dairy" one unexcelled on the coast. With 300 cows yielding an average of 275 pounds of butter daily, the buildings of the ranch resemble a small village. Water brought from a mountain reservoir 8,000 feet distant, with 220 feet fall, furnishes power for the cream separators and various other machinery, beside running a one-hundred light dynamo by which all the buildings and yards are lighted. The raising of horses, swine and thoroughbred poultry is also an important adjunct.

He married, Oct. 13, 1867, MARANDA FLORENZA FINCH,* dau. of

---

* Maranda F. Shippy m., 1st, Mar. 23, 1851, Isaac S. Finch, son of Isaac R. Finch and Hannah Towileger. He was born in Niles, Mich., Mar. 5, 1830, and died in Hagar, Mich., May 23, 1858, aged 28.

CHILDREN.
1. *Charles William*, b. Feb. 8, 1852; m. Mar. 31, 1874, Abbie Louisa Merrill.
2. *Madison Frederick*, b. Feb. 10, 1854; m. Apr. 15, 1877, Ada Eloise Merrill.

William Shippy and Lydia Ingram, and widow of Isaac S. Finch. She was born in Watertown, N. Y., Sept 2, 1831.

CHILDREN.

1. *Deloss Burton,* b. Aug. 20, 1868.
2. *Melvin Dwight,* b. Mar. 24, 1875.

---

83. SUSAN WILDER, dau. of Calvin Wilder and Phebe Wilder, (74), was born in Hartland, Conn., Aug. 20, 1830. She resides in Riverton, Conn.

She married, Jan. 1, 1850, WATSON EMERSON FRENCH. (See Family 80.)

CHILDREN.

1. *Leroy Emerson,*   b. Oct. 13, 1850; m. Mary A. Kerwood.   (82)
2. *William Carrosso,* b. Mar. 4, 1852;   m. Marilla A. Richardson; Carrie
                                              [L. Smith.   (93)
3. *Emerson Watson,*   b. Mar. 24, 1854; d. Apr. 2, 1854.
4. *Deloss Dwight,*   b. Mar. 21, 1855; m. Mary E. Richardson.   (94)
5. *Horace Wilder,*   b. Aug. 13, 1860; m. Fannie E. Moxley.   (95)

---

84. LAROYAL TAYLOR, son of Lester Taylor and Mary L. Wilder, (75), was born in Claridon, Ohio, May 27, 1827. He enlisted in the U. S. Navy in 1849 and served three years and four months on the ship "Independence," of the Mediterranean squadron. It was a time of peace and he never saw any engagement. Acting as Past-Midshipman's Steward, he spent much time on shore and visited all the countries and cities on that sea. His roving disposition satisfied, he returned home, married and settled down to farm life. He enlisted in Company E, 105th Regiment, Ohio Volunteer Infantry, in Aug., 1862, and was first Sergeant. The review at Louisville, Ky., with the mercury at 100 degrees in the shade, followed soon after by the retreat from Bragg's army, sent him to the hospital. He rejoined his regiment but was discharged for disability May 16, 1863, having seen little active service. He never fully recovered his health. He lives near Willoughby, Ohio.

He married, May 18, 1854, ANNA BUTLER CLEVELAND, dau. of Dr. John Smith Cleveland and Chloe Butler. She was born in Akron, Ohio, Oct. 31, 1836.

CHILDREN.

1. *Innetta Sophia,* b. Mar. 26, 1855; m. H. A. Rice; T. V. Stockton. (96)
2. *Royal Cleveland,* b. June 24, 1857; m. Sylvia J. Pike. (97)
3. *Ella Cook,*   b. June 18, 1861; m. Fred E. Presley. (98)
4. *John Wilder,*   b. Dec. 18, 1866; d. Jan. 1, 1897, ae. 30.
5. *Mary Alice,*   b. Sept. 17, 1870; m. Van Deusen Farquharson. (99)

85. LESTER DEWITT TAYLOR, son of Lester Taylor and Mary L. Wilder, (75), was born in Claridon, Ohio, Dec. 1, 1832. He was a farmer, and in Aug., 1862, he enlisted in the 105th reg., Ohio Volunteer Infantry, with his brother LaRoyal; was promoted to be Sergeant Major, and was in many battles, the first, Perryville, soon after reaching Kentucky. He was at Lookout Mountain, the siege of Atlanta, and went with Sherman to the sea. He was never in a hospital, and the regiment was never transported by rail, but always marched, and he felt, with reason, that very few were in the army so long and came out so well as he.

After the close of the war he returned to farm life near Claridon. He was a director of the Thompson Mutual Fire Insurance Company for several terms. As county commissioner he was serving his second term when he died, June 6, 1891, aged 58.

He married, Sept. 29, 1868, CARMELIA BRAINARD, dau. of Nelson Brainard and Lucia Rudd. She was born in Parma, Ohio, Nov. 19, 1843. She resides in Cleveland, Ohio.

CHILDREN.

1. *Wilder Brainard,* b. Sept. 16, 1869; m. Marietta E. Rowley. (100)
2. *Arthur Wallace,* b. Mar. 14, 1872; is a mining engineer, lives in Cleve-
   [land, Ohio.

86. LUCY WILDER TAYLOR, dau. of Lester Taylor and Mary L. Wilder, (75), was born in Claridon, Ohio, Aug. 19, 1835.

She married, May 31, 1859, CLINTON GOODWIN, son of Emery Goodwin and Mary French King. He was born in New Hartford, Conn., Jan. 29, 1830. His mother was named after Mary French, an ancestor, who when about ten years old was taken captive by the French and Indians at Deerfield, Mass., and carried to Canada. She afterwards married, and to show her children how she lived in captivity caused them to dig and eat ground nuts. His grandfather, Asa Goodwin, was one of the most prominent of the early settlers of New Hartford, having held the office of town clerk for forty years and served several terms in the legislature. His father was active in assisting fugitive slaves to reach Canada in slavery days, keeping a depot on the "Underground Railroad," as it was termed.

In 1835 his parents emigrated to Geauga County, Ohio, and settled in the town of Burton, and the next year moved to Middlefield, in that county, where he attended the common school and was nine months at the West Farmington academy. When twenty-one he taught school for three years in central and northern Ohio. In 1857 he went to Kansas, and became a land-holder, but returned to Middlefield in 1859, and four years later moved to a farm two miles north of Center Claridon, where he now lives. He has served as deacon in the Congregational church.

CHILDREN.

1. *Florence Isidore,* b. Aug. 12, 1860; m. George A. Bartholomew. (101)
2. *Mary Catherine,* b. Feb. 23, 1863; is a physician in Warren, Ohio.
3. *Lester Taylor,* b. Dec. 22, 1865; is a dentist in Claridon.
4. *Emery Milton,* b. Mar. 30, 1868; is a physician in Cleveland, Ohio.
5. *Lucy Lenora,* b. June 6, 1871; m. Emmet J. Strong. (102)

---

87. JANE SOPHIA TAYLOR, dau. of Lester Taylor and Mary L. Wilder, (75), was born in Claridon, Ohio, Nov. 23, 1837, and died in Barrington, Ill., Jan. 30, 1866, aged 28.

She married, Jan. 1, 1863, WILLIAM DAVID RINGLAND,* son of William Ringland and Sarah Babbett. He was born in Amherst, Ohio, June 19, 1839, was educated in Oberlin, Ohio, and then commenced life in the mercantile business, continuing until 1873, when he became editor and publisher of the "New Era," at Woodstock.

* W. D. Ringland married, 2nd, Oct. 23, 1866, Amanda Malvina Matthews, dau. of John Matthews and Rachel McFarlin. She was born in Montville, Ohio, Aug. 4, 1843.

CHILDREN.

1. *Rachel Anne,* b. Sept. 26, 1867.
2. *Lillys Margaret,* b. Apr. 8, 1869.
3. *Wilbur David,* b. July 31, 1880.

III. After ten years of literary work he again engaged in mercantile life and now resides in Kasson, Minn.

CHILDREN.

1. *Effie Jane*, b. Feb. 23, 1864; d. May 7, 1880, ae. 16.
2. *Heman Lester*, b. Aug. 19, 1865.

---

88. SUSAN ROSEBOOM TAYLOR, dau. of Lester Taylor and Mary L. Wilder, (75), was born in Claridon, Ohio, Apr. 16, 1841.

She married, Jan. 1, 1863, OZRO ROBINSON NEWCOMB, son of Orrin Newcomb and Permelia Robinson. He was born in Parkman, Ohio, July 21, 1834, being one of twelve children. It was a strange fancy of his parents to give each a name beginning with O, as follows: Otis, Ormand, Orrella, Olive, Orris, Orlen, Orriann, Orriett, Orlando, Orren, Ozro and Orlo. His mother was a lineal descendant of Rev. John Robinson, the first pastor of Plymouth Colony, and Mr. Newcomb was the eighth descendant in direct line. He was a farmer and at the time of his marriage was Treasurer of Geauga county, and was serving a second term when he died in Chardon, Ohio, Jan. 1, 1866, aged 31.

CHILD.

Ozro Robinson, Jr., b. July 21, 1866: is a Congregational minister.

---

89. MARY LOUISA FRENCH, dau. of Watson E. French and Mary L. Wilder, (80), was born in Winsted, Conn., Sept. 2, 1846, and died in Hartland, Conn., Sept. 28, 1877, aged 31.

She married, Mar. 14, 1867, GEORGE HENRY RANSBOTHAN,* son of Thomas Ransbothan and Ellen Ward. He was born in Hartland, Aug. 23, 1842, and was a farmer there until Apr. 1, 1892, when he moved to Riverton, Conn., where he died Sept. 15, 1895, aged 53.

CHILD.

Hattie Mary, b. Apr. 22, 1870; m. William H. Griswold. (103)

---

* G. H. Ransbothan married, 2nd, June 15, 1892, Nellie Louise Gates, dau. of John Fay Gates and Mary Jane Catlin. She was born in Hartford, Conn., July 13, 1858.

CHILD.

Kenneth Gates, b. Sept. 23, 1893; d. Jan. 7, 1895, ae. 1.

90. ORVILLE HOWD WILDER, son of Austin J. Wilder and Marinda Pickett, (81), was born in Jefferson, N. Y., June 3, 1857. In the spring of 1879 he went to California, and is associated with his uncle in the "Wilder Dairy," near Santa Cruz, in that state.

He married, Aug. 27, 1882, CARRIE FRANCES MERRILL, dau. of Sylvester Merrill and Louisa A. Merrill. She was born in Wentworth, N. H., Nov. 13, 1863.

CHILDREN.

1. *Mabel Louisa*, b. July 31, 1883.
2. *Edna Marinda*, b. Feb. 25, 1885.
3. *Leland Austin*, b. July 19, 1888.
4. *Roy Sylvester*, b. Aug. 25, 1890.
5. *Arlie May*, b. Apr. 25, 1895.

---

91. PHEBE ELIZABETH WILDER, dau. of Austin J. Wilder and Mary H. Thomas, (81), was born in Jefferson, N. Y., Feb. 3, 1874.

She married, Mar. 25, 1896, FRANK HOAGLAND, son of Martin Hoagland and Lucinda Slater. He was born in Eastkill, N. Y., Oct. 22, 1868. He is a farmer, and lives near Stamford, N. Y.

---

92. LEROY EMERSON FRENCH, son of Watson E. French and Susan Wilder, (83), was born in West Hartland, Conn., Oct. 13, 1850. He is a farmer and lives about three miles north-east of Riverton, Conn.

He married, Sept. 3, 1874, MARY JANE KERWOOD, dau. of Walter Kerwood and Mary Ann Price. She was born in New Hartford, Conn., Mar. 12, 1859.

CHILD.

Jessie Belle, b. Aug. 22, 1875; m. Burton J. Ford. (104)

---

93. WILLIAM CARVOSSO FRENCH, son of Watson E. French and Susan Wilder, (83), was born in West Hartland, Conn., Mar. 4, 1852. He is a farmer, and lives two and one-half miles north-east of Riverton, Conn.

He married, 1st, Apr. 29, 1874, MARILLA ANNA RICHARDSON, dau. of Rollin R. Richardson and Harriet Almena Smith. She was born in Hartland, Conn., Nov. 15, 1854, and died there, June 10, 1883, aged 28, leaving no children.

He married, 2nd, Dec. 24, 1885, CARRIE LOUISA SMITH, dau. of Edgar Smith and Betsey Seeley Ferry. She was born in Norwalk, Conn., Nov. 16, 1859.

CHILDREN:— by the second marriage.

1. *Susan Betsey*,   b. Oct. 3, 1886.
2. *Edgar Watson*,   b. Jan. 1, 1888.
3. *Harold Carrosso*,   b. July 14, 1889.
4. *Calvin Wilder*,   b. May 5, 1891.
5. *Christina Louisa*, b. Feb. 14, 1895.

---

94. DELOSS DWIGHT FRENCH, son of Watson E. French and Susan Wilder, (83), was born in West Hartland, Conn., Mar. 21, 1855. He is a farmer, and lives one and one-half miles east of New Hartford, Conn.

He married, Apr. 29, 1874, MARY ELLEN RICHARDSON, dau. of Rollin R. Richardson and Harriet Almena Smith. She was born in Hartland, Conn., Sept. 18, 1858.

CHILDREN.

By adoption, *Hattie Belle*, b. June 1, 1876.
1. *Milton Wellington*,   b. Nov. 6, 1884.
2. *Harold Richardson*,   b. May 19, 1890.
3. *Mildred May*,   b. Nov. 1, 1896.

---

95. HORACE WILDER FRENCH, son of Watson E. French and Susan Wilder, (83), was born in Hartland, Conn., Aug. 13, 1860. He lives in Waterbury, Conn., and is an employee in the Waterbury Clock Company.

He married, Dec. 23, 1880, FANNIE ETHEL MOXLEY, dau. of Henry Moxley and Mary Ann Stephens. She was born in Newport, Monmouthshire, England, Apr. 13, 1857.

CHILDREN.

1. *Harry Beardslee*, b. May 9, 1881.
2. *Bessie Moxley*,   b. Feb. 23, 1885; d. Aug. 9, 1885.
3. *Elsie May*,   b. Feb. 23, 1885.
4. *Leroy Emerson*,   b. May 26, 1888.
5. *Hazel Wilder*,   b. June 26, 1890.

96. ANNETTA SOPHIA TAYLOR, dau. of LaRoyal Taylor and Anna B. Cleveland, (84), was born in Claridon, Ohio, Mar. 26, 1855.

She married, 1st, Oct. 16, 1879, HERBERT ALFRED RICE, son of Porter Rice and Lydia B. Tuller. He was born in Pleasant Valley, Ohio, Aug. 15, 1855. He was a contractor and builder and possessed excellent business qualities and energy. He died in Willoughby, Ohio, Jan. 29, 1891, aged 35, leaving no children.

She married, 2nd, Mar. 29, 1894, THOMAS VANCE STOCKTON, son of Robert Stockton and Rebecca Wilson. He was born in the town of Franklin, Penn., Dec. 12, 1845, graduating from Washington College, Penn., and Merchant's College, and is a farmer, living three miles west of Washington, Penn.

---

97. ROYAL CLEVELAND TAYLOR, son of LaRoyal Taylor and Anna B. Cleveland, (84), was born in Claridon, Ohio, June 24, 1857. He is a farmer and lives about three miles south of Willoughby, Ohio.

He married, Aug. 22, 1883, SYLVIA JANE PIKE, dau. of John Dwight Pike and Mabel Lorinda Gray. She was born in Mayfield, Ohio, June 3, 1859.

CHILDREN.
1. *Mary Wilder*, b. July 27, 1884.
2. *Lester LaRoyal*, b. Apr. 6, 1892.

---

98. ELLA COOK TAYLOR, dau. of LaRoyal Taylor and Anna B. Cleveland, (84), was born in Claridon, Ohio, June 18, 1861.

She married, May 24, 1882, FRED EUGENE PRESLEY, son of Solomon Presley and Emma Eliza Hayford. He was born in Chester, Ohio, Sept. 19, 1860. He is a farmer in Kirtland township, two miles from Willoughby, Ohio.

JOHN WILDER TAYLOR, son of LaRoyal Taylor and Anna B. Cleveland, (84), was born in Claridon, Ohio, Dec. 18, 1866. He attended the Willoughby High School, followed by four years at the Ohio State University, where he studied civil engineering. In 1891 he located in Troy, Ohio, and became City Engineer, making a most efficient officer. He was a member of the Presbyterian church, and an earnest worker in the Christian Endeavor Society. In Feb., 1896, ill health compelled him to seek a milder clime and he went to Hagerman, New Mexico, but that dread disease, consumption, was too firmly fastened, and he died there, Jan. 1, 1897, aged 30. His remains were taken to Willoughby, where his youngest sister had died the following day, and both were interred in the Waite Hill cemetery.

99. MARY ALICE TAYLOR, dau. of LaRoyal Taylor and Anna B. Cleveland, (84), was born in Willoughby, Ohio, Sept. 17, 1870. She was a member of the Presbyterian church, a true christian and a most affectionate wife and mother. She died in Willoughby, Jan. 2, 1897, aged 26.

She married, Dec. 31, 1891, VAN DEUSEN FARQUHARSON, son of James Henry Farquharson and Marion Hale. He was born in Allegany, N. Y., Feb. 2, 1872, and is a mechanic.

CHILDREN.

1. *Daisy*, b. May 23, 1893.
2. *Donald*, b. July 1, 1896.

100. WILDER BRAINARD TAYLOR, son of Lester D. Taylor and Carmelia Brainard, (85), was born in Claridon, Ohio, Sept. 16, 1869. He was a farmer and cattle dealer, and lived one mile northwest of Claridon, where he died Sept. 7, 1897, aged nearly 28.

He married, Dec. 24, 1889, MARIETTA ELECTA ROWLEY, dau. of Sherwood Allen Rowley and Elosia Andrews. She was born in Claridon, Dec. 31, 1867, where she now lives.

CHILD.

Robert Lester, b. Jan. 16, 1894.

ARTHUR WALLACE TAYLOR, son of Lester D. Taylor and Carmelia Brainard, (85), was born in Claridon, Ohio, Mar. 14, 1872. He attended the high School at Chardon and graduated in 1889, then entered the Ohio State University, at Columbus, and graduated in mining and metallurgy in 1893, receiving the degree of Engineer of Mines. He is an analytical chemist in Cleveland, Ohio.

101. FLORENCE ISIDORE GOODWIN, dau. of Clinton Goodwin and Lucy W. Taylor, (86), was born in Middlefield, Ohio. Aug. 12, 1860.

She married, May 31, 1881, GEORGE ALBA BARTHOLOMEW, son of George Washington Bartholomew, and Angeline Elizabeth Houghton. He was born in Welshfield, Ohio, Apr. 20, 1857. He is a farmer and lives near Huntsburg, Ohio.

CHILDREN.

1. *Robb Ozro*, b. Nov. 1, 1882.
2. *Mary Angeline*, b. Oct. 1, 1890.

Dr. MARY CATHERINE GOODWIN, dau. of Clinton Goodwin and Lucy W. Taylor, (86), was born in Middlefield, Ohio, Feb. 23, 1863. She attended the high school at Chardon, where she graduated in 1884. Until 1893 her time was occupied in teaching, and that year she began the study of medicine, graduating from the Cleveland College of Physicians and Surgeons, in Mar., 1897. She practices her profession in Warren, Ohio.

102. LUCY LENORA GOODWIN, dau. of Clinton Goodwin and Lucy W. Taylor, (86), was born in Claridon, Ohio, June 6, 1871.

She married, June 7, 1893, EMMET JOSEPH STRONG, son of Lyman Strong and Lydia Curtis. He was born in Huntsburg, Ohio, Jan. 31, 1862. He is a member of the Curtis Steel Roofing Co., manufacturers of Iron and Steel Roofing and Siding, Niles. Ohio.

CHILD.

Lester Lyman, b. Jan. 30, 1895.

103. HATTIE MARY RANSBOTHAN, dau. of George H. Ransbotham and Mary L. French, (89), was born in Hartland, Conn., Apr. 22, 1870.

She married, Nov. 14, 1894, WILLIAM HENRY GRISWOLD, son of Henry Herbert Griswold and Annie Perces Gaylord. He was born in Hartland, Dec. 13, 1867, and is a bookkeeper. He lived in Torrington, Conn., until Oct. 17, 1895, when he moved to Dalton, Mass., where he now resides.

---

104. JESSIE BELLE FRENCH, dau. of Leroy E. French and Mary J. Kerwood, (92), was born in Thomaston, Conn., Aug. 22, 1875.

She married, Jan. 15, 1896, BURTON JAY FORD, son of Jay A. Ford and Turzey Finette Granger. He was born in Torrington, Conn., Jan. 24, 1868. He lives in Torrington, and is a mechanic.

CHILD.

Ruth Irene, b. May 21, 1897.

LUCY JOHNSON KENNEDY.

105. LUCY JOHNSON, dau. of Jesse Johnson and Mary Stevenson, (10), was born in Chatham, Conn., May 3, 1781, and died in Cherry Valley, N. Y., Aug. 13, 1806, aged 25.

She married, 1804, Dr. JAMES KENNEDY,* son of Robert Kennedy and Jane Pratt. He was born Apr. 12, 1773. The Kennedy family trace their ancestry back to Robert the Bruce, and the name Robert occurs very frequently in all their family records. James was the eldest of eleven children, four of the five sons being physicians. The family probably emigrated from Mass. to Central New York about the beginning of the present century. He studied medicine with Dr. Joseph White, in Cherry Valley, and practiced that profession in Little Falls, N. Y. After the death of his second wife he went west and further information concerning him has been unattainable.

CHILD.

Robert Johnson, b. Jan. 12, 1806: d. Aug. 23, 1806.

---

* Dr. Kennedy married, 2nd, Sept. 30, 1808, Lucy Johnson, dau. of Ozias Wilcox and Mabel Gould, and widow of Robert Johnson. (See Family 50.)

CHILD.

Sophia Aurora, b. June 1, 1811; m. 1831, Rev. Henry Snyder; d. Jan. 21, 1832, ae. 20.

SALLY MARIA JOHNSON AND DESCENDANTS.

106. SALLY MARIA JOHNSON, dau. of Jesse Johnson and Mary Stevenson, (10), was born in Chatham, Conn., Sept. 13, 1783. She was a bright ornament to society and filled the position to which the prominence of her husband raised her, with dignity and grace. It was to her, by inheritance as well as thorough training, that some of the conspicuous qualities were due which distinguished her eminent daughter, Mrs. Lord.

On Dec. 30, 1813, when the village of Buffalo was, with the exception of two houses, burned by the British and Indians, she escaped to Williamsville with her infant, but returned as soon as personal safety was assured. Then followed extreme hardships. An extract from a letter written by a sister-in-law, dated May 29, 1814, says: "I have the week past received a letter from sister Sally in which she says they are once more in a house of their own, but that they lived for a time without floor, door or window. She has kept house for three months with three knives and forks, one tea cup, three custard cups and five earthen plates, which was all she saved of her crockery. She had saved her beds and bedding but that was the principle part of their property that they did save. Her looking-glass and some other articles she had been obliged to sell towards procuring some things to make their home habitable."

"She was a sincere and devoted christian; by a life of active benevolence she furnished that proof of the power and reality of religion which neither can be refuted nor evaded by the cavils of the skeptics:" so reads her obituary, adding the following high tribute to her gracious character: "The poor of this city have lost a benefactress, the extent of whose beneficence and the multitude of whose charities will never be fully known in time; while the rich have lost the example of one who used wealth, not in fashionable display, but in advancing every good work, and aiding all those benevolent institutions which have for their object the amelioration of the condition of man and the glory of God." She died in Buffalo, Mar. 7, 1834, aged 50.

She married, Jan. 25, 1811, Dr. EBENEZER JOHNSON,* son of Capt. Ebenezer Johnson and Deborah Lathrop. He was born in Conn., Nov. 7, 1786. He was a student of the eminent Dr. Joseph White, of Cherry Valley, N. Y., and in 1809 went to Buffalo, where he practiced his profession until the second war with Great Britain broke out in 1812, when he entered the service of his country as army surgeon. He engaged in the drug business for a time and then became a partner of Judge Wilkinson's for a few years, acquiring considerable wealth as a banker and broker. He was one of the founders of the larger fortunes of Buffalo, and when the city was incorporated in 1832, he was chosen its first mayor. "The Cottage" and "Park," as his mansion and grounds were known, were long landmarks of the earlier splendor of its private life, and this sort of baronial home of the family marked the boundery between the native forest and the incipient city. He died in Tellico Plains, Tenn., Feb. 8, 1848, aged 61.

CHILDREN.

1. *Mary Elizabeth,* b. Jan. 6, 1812; m. Rev. John C. Lord. (107)
2. *William Henry* b. Apr. 25, 1816; m. Mary A. Wheeler. (108)
3. *Sarah Maria,* b. Feb. 22, 1821; m. Dr. Smith Inglehart. (109)

---

107. MARY ELIZABETH JOHNSON, dau. of Dr. Ebenezer Johnson and Sally M. Johnson, (106), was born in Buffalo, N. Y., Jan. 6, 1812, when the place was a mere hamlet. She was educated at

---

* Dr. Johnson married, 2nd, Dec. 7, 1835, Lucy Elizabeth Lord, dau. of John Way Lord and Sarah Chase. She was born in Morrisville, N. Y., Mar. 20, 1814, and died in Geneseo, N. Y., Nov. 30, 1850, aged 36.

CHILDREN.

1. *Herbert Lord,* b. Jan. 4, 1837; m. June 20, 1860, Amelia Greene.
2. *Sarah Cecilia,* b. July 25, 1840; m. July 29, 1863, Horace Utley.
3. *Sarah Louisa,* b. July 12, 1846; d. 1849.

Mrs. Willard's school in Troy, N. Y., and at a reception given to LaFayette she had the honor of being kissed by the Marquis as being the least of the school girls. She was undoubtedly one of the most remarkable women our country has ever produced. She held a position of affluence and influence in her parents' attractive home, and it was there that John C. Lord, then a young lawyer of ambition, met and won her. In the midst of a party at "The Cottage," she eloped, leaving on her bureau an earnest of that keen wit and never failing brightness which distinguished her among women throughout her long life, in the shape of a note to her parents that deserves to head the long list of such interesting missives, for the would-be Mrs. Lord simply wrote: "The Lord gave, and the Lord hath taken away; blessed be the name of the Lord." The Lord Library, now in the custody of the Historical Society, could not have said more.

She was, an original character of peculiar and very steadfast aims, and although the playful saying was attributed to her, that she had married a lawyer and not a clergyman, and could not be held to the responsibilities of a pastor's wife, by her own peculiar methods she adapted herself to the new position, bringing to it a warm heart and boundless sympathy, and, without regulative conformities, gave free play to a nature as original as it was generous and loyal. Her wit and humor, at times approaching grotesqueness, was never dissociated from sympathy with every form of suffering in man or beast.

The crown of her character was her intense and peculiar development of humanitarianism, if such may be called a tenderness of compassion whose objects were especially the brutes dependent on the care of mankind. The brutal teamster feared her, but could not escape the ingenious expedients by which she extorted justice if she could not mercy. The unfeeling urchin preferred to forego his coveted enjoyment of torturing poor animals to enduring the punishment of her wit. Long before the world had heard of Henry Bergh, she was in herself a whole society for the prevention of cruelty to animals. While for this trait she bore the "diploma of honor" of the Humane Society of Turin, Italy, she supported steadfastly every project for the alleviation of human suffering and did much to advance the cure of their souls. Willing to sit it out for hours by a curb-stone contesting the question of a horse's rights against his driver, she could identify herself with an ex-President in organizing a society, interest herself in founding an orphan asylum, and equally find a field for religious services for the benefit of the unchurched on her own lawn.

"Religious without bigotry, pious without cant, she enjoyed the good of life until she could no longer act her part, and then had no longer a wish to live, but with no morbid feeling, and in a spirit of true religious resignation she recognized a philosophic fitness in the order of life and death." Her six-horse team of Shetland ponies was long a feature of Buffalo, and her quaint little figure and determined energy were deeply regretted and long missed after her death. She died in Buffalo, May 26, 1885, aged 73, leaving no children.

She married, Dec. 9, 1828, Rev. JOHN CHASE LORD, son of Rev. John Way Lord and Sarah Chase. He was born in Washington, N. H., Aug. 9, 1805. When he was five years of age his parents moved to Burlington, Otsego Co., N. Y. He was sent to school at Plainfield, N. H., and received part of his preparatory education at the academy which has since become Madison college. In 1822 he entered Hamilton college, where he passed two years, his ambition for active life then impelling him to attempt the editorship of a paper, "The Canadian," in which he spent two years with small advantage.

In 1825 he entered upon the study of law at Buffalo, then a village of 2500 inhabitants. In that year the Erie canal was completed and the prosperity of the place became assured. He helped to make his way by teaching an academy and as deputy county clerk, and was admitted to the Bar in 1828. The parents of his intended wife objected to his marriage at this time on account of their daughter's youthful age, but became his firm supporters and friends through a long lifetime. The question of a religious life was agitating his mind at the same time, which was settled by his determination not only to unite with the church but to become a minister. Not content with his already considerable education and attainments,— he had given the semi-centennial address at the celebration of the founding of Buffalo, in the first year of his residence there,— his thorough going disposition made him determine upon a complete theological preparation. He entered Auburn Seminary in 1831 and graduated two years later. For a few months he preached in Fayetteville, N. Y., and then labored in Genesco, N. Y., until 1835, when he was induced to undertake the new enterprise of a colony from the First Presbyterian

Church of Buffalo, then worshipping in a temporary building, and whose first edifice was called the Pearl Street Church. The large and important edifice which took the name of the Central Church was completed in 1852. (In that year he was Moderator of the General Assembly at Charleston, S. C.)

Here his wonderful efforts were heard, from time to time with especial eloquence and power upon topics of extraordinary interest, till 1870, his labors being greatly blessed, more than a thousand members being received into the church during his pastorate. Then he had an assistant for a time, but finally retired in 1873, and passed his remaining years in honored leisure and domestic peace, surrounded by his books in his grand library, among the valuable and antique curios from all parts of the world, which were devised later to the city of Buffalo. As a writer he published " Lectures to Young Men," " Lectures on Civilization," etc., a volume of occasional poems, beside a great number of sermons, essays and contributions to periodicals. He died in Buffalo, Jan. 22, 1877, aged 71.

CHILD:— by adoption.

Frances Johnson,* b. Nov. 7, 1828; m. William C. Sherwood.

---

108. WILLIAM HENRY JOHNSON, son of Dr. Ebenzer Johnson and Sally M. Johnson. (106), was born in Buffalo, N. Y., Apr. 25, 1816. He was a graduate of Union College, and a civil engineer by profession. He afterwards became a farmer in Fredonia, N. Y., where he died in May, 1845, aged 29.

He married, Dec. 25, 1838, MARY ANNE WHEELER,† dau. of

---

* Frances J. Lord married, Sept. 14, 1844, William Charles Sherwood, son of John Adiel Sherwood, and Anna Mary Adams. He was born in Orangeville, N. Y., Feb. 10, 1813.

CHILDREN.

1. *Mary Lord*, b. June 6, 1845; d. Aug. 6, 1846, ae. 1.
2. *William Lord*, b. Nov. 3, 1847; d. Apr. 14, 1873, ae. 25.
3. *John Chase*, b. Oct. 25, 1854; m. Feb. 17, 1886, Louise Isett Madeira.

† Mrs. Johnson married, 2nd, May 30, 1852, John Charles Gray, son of William Gray and Hannah Maidman. He was born in London, England, Dec. 28, 1815, and died in St. Louis, Mo., July 23, 1896, aged 80.

CHILDREN.

1. *John Henry*, b. June 8, 1853; m. Apr. 13, 1885, Lizzie Hold.
2. *Bessie*, b. Oct. 24, 1855.
3. *Nellie*, b. July 18, 1857; m. Sept. 1, 1881, Frank Samuel Chandler; Jan. 26, [1888, Dr. Waldo Briggs.
4. *Winnie*, b. Apr. 16, 1860.
5. *Mary Wilma*, b. May 27, 1865.

William F. Wheeler and Susan Conant. She was born in New York City, Nov. 5, 1820, and died in Centralia, Ill., Sept. 4. 1887, aged 66.

CHILDREN.

1. *Charles Ernest,* b. Aug. 27, 1840.
2. *William Sherwood,* b. May 12, 1844; m. Kate F. Richards. (110)

---

109. SARAH MARIA JOHNSON, dau. of Dr. Ebenezer Johnson and Sally M. Johnson, (106), was born in Buffalo, N. Y., Feb. 22, 1821, and died in Glenville, near Cleveland, Ohio, Nov. 13, 1852, aged 31.

She married, Jan. 22, 1842, Dr. SMITH INGLEHART, son of Ira Inglehart and Elizabeth VanWaters. He was born in Houndsfield, near Watertown, N. Y., Oct. 1, 1815. When a young man he went to Cleveland, and entered the employ of a druggist, then studied medicine and practiced that profession until the spring of 1845, when he was appointed Collector of the Port, in that city, by Pres. James K. Polk, which office he filled for two years, and then engaged in farming in Glenville, a suburb of Cleveland. In 1870 he returned to the city and entered mercantile business. He died there, Feb. 14, 1871, aged 55.

CHILDREN.

1. *Maria Johnson,* b. Nov. 21, 1842; d. July 22, 1843.
2. *Mary Johnson,* b. Oct. 8, 1845; d. June 19, 1846.
3. *George Nelson,* b. Dec. 28, 1847; m. Margaret Cuthbertson. (111)
4. *Fred May,* b. Feb. 9, 1851; m. Lizzie Stevens. (112)
5. *Maria Smith,* b. June 20, 1852; m. James B. Gill. (113)

---

110. WILLIAM SHERWOOD JOHNSON, son of William H. Johnson and Mary A. Wheeler, (108), was born in Fredonia, N. Y., May 12, 1844. He is in the mercantile business, and lives in San Francisco, Cal.

He married, Aug. 28, 1877, KATE FRANCES RICHARDS, dau. of James Martin Richards and Ann Melissa Butterworth. She was born in Wellsburgh, Va., Dec. 22, 1855.

CHILDREN.

1. *Sherwood,* b. Apr. 4, 1879; d. Nov. 25, 1879.
2. *Katharine,* b. Jan. 21, 1882.

111. GEORGE NELSON INGLEHART, son of Dr. Smith Inglehart and Sarah M. Johnson, (109), was born in Cleveland, Ohio, Dec. 28, 1847. He was educated in the public schools and at Shaw academy, in East Cleveland. He is a book-keeper for the Union Drop Forge Company, Chicago, Ill.

He married, Apr. 25, 1872, MARGARET CUTHBERTSON, dau. of James Cuthbertson and Margaret Billsland. She was born in Guilderland, N. Y., Aug. 19, 1847.

CHILDREN.

1. *Edwin Smith,* b. Aug. 23, 1873.
2. *Mary Johnson,* b. Jan. 20, 1878.

112. FRED MAY INGLEHART, son of Dr. Smith Inglehart and Sarah M. Johnson, (109), was born in Glenville, near Cleveland, Ohio, Feb. 9, 1851. He attended the high school in the city for some years and then entered the Collegiate Department of the University of Michigan, at Ann Arbor, where he graduated. He commenced the study of law in Buffalo, residing with his aunt, Mrs. John C. Lord. He entered the office of Lyman K. Bass and Grover Cleveland, and was managing clerk for five years. He was admitted to the Bar in 1873, but remained with his preceptors some time longer. With the exception of a partnership of four years with Morris Morey, he has had no associate in business.

He married, Oct. 3, 1878, LIZZIE STEVENS, dau. of Elias Rhaum and Margaret Elizabeth Humason, and adopted dau. of Milo Stevens and Julia Elmira Humason. She was born in Windsor Locks, Conn., Feb. 15, 1856.

CHILDREN.

1. *Robert Stevens,* b. July 13, 1879.
2. *Frederick Johnson,* b. May 28, 1881.
3. *Julia Elizabeth,* b. Apr. 2, 1888.
4. *Milo,* b. Aug. 14, 1890.

113. MARIA SMITH INGLEHART, dau. of Dr. Smith Inglehart and Sarah M. Johnson, (109), was born in Glenville, Ohio, June 20, 1852. She resides in Cleveland.

She married, May 19, 1874, JAMES BENJAMIN GILL, son of Robert Gill and Josephine Manning. He was born in Troy, N. Y., Feb. 14, 1850.

CHILDREN.

1. *James Garrett,* b. Mar. 7, 1875; d. Aug. 13, 1875.
2. *Grace Hattie,* b. Mar. 25, 1876; m. George Hessert. (114)
3. *Walter Scott,* b. Aug. 10, 1878; d. Dec. 24, 1879, ae. 1.
4. *May Nellie,* b. May 10, 1880; d. May 13, 1881, ae. 1.

---

114. GRACE HATTIE GILL, dau. of James B. Gill and Maria S. Inglehart, (113), was born in Sacramento, Cal., Mar. 25, 1876.

She married, Mar. 29, 1894, GEORGE HESSERT, son of Adam Hessert and Kate Wermerskircher. He was born in Rockport, Ohio, Sept. 16, 1871. He is a mechanic, and lives in Cleveland, Ohio.

CHILD.

Gladys Inglehart, b. Jan. 27, 1895.

ERASTUS JOHNSON AND DESCENDANTS.

115. ERASTUS JOHNSON, son of Jesse Johnson and Mary Stevenson, (10), was born in Chatham, Conn., Apr. 10, 1786. He came with his parents to the town of Cherry Valley, N. Y., in 1804, and assisted his father on the farm, although long continued ill-health prevented his taking part in active labor. Upon the death of the latter in 1832 he inherited the homestead which subsequently passed into the possession of the Campbell family and is now known as "Oakwood." In Apr., 1835, he moved to the village of Cherry Valley where he died, Mar. 25, 1837, aged nearly 51.

He married, Apr. 9, 1809, JERUSHA WILLIAMS HOLT, dau. of Gen. Elijah Holt and Elizabeth Williams. She was born in Cherry Valley, Jan. 20, 1791, and died in that town, Dec. 2, 1834, aged 43.

CHILDREN.

1. Robert Holt, b. May 5, 1811; d. Aug. 1, 1834, ae. 23; gored to [death by a bull.
2. Elizabeth Williams, b. Nov. 16, 1812; d. Apr. 7, 1815, ae. 2.
3. Mary Stevenson, b. May 11, 1815; m. James B. Dunlap. (116)
4. Sarah Williams, b. June 5, 1820; m. Dr. Smith Inglehart. (117)
5. Cynthia Eliza, b. July 1, 1824; m. John Judd. (118)
6. Lucy Maria, b. Feb. 26, 1828; d. Mar. 29, 1844, ae. 16.

---

116. MARY STEVENSON JOHNSON, dau. of Erastus Johnson and Jerusha W. Holt, (115), was born in the town of Cherry Valley, N. Y., May 11, 1815, and died in that village, Jan. 6, 1842, aged 26, leaving no children.

She married, May 23, 1839, JAMES BUTLER DUNLAP,* son of Robert Dunlap and Hannah Burkitt. He was born in Cherry Valley, Dec. 9, 1814. He was educated in the academy, and then was associated with his father in mercantile business. In 1848 he moved to Milwaukee, Wis., and engaged in the drug business. During the war he was employed in the post-office department, at Washington, D. C., for two years. He died in Milwaukee, Dec. 8, 1872, aged 58.

---

117. SARAH WILLIAMS JOHNSON, dau. of Erastus Johnson and Jerusha W. Holt, (115), was born in the town of Cherry Valley, N. Y., June 5, 1820. She resides in Buffalo, N. Y.

She married, June 15, 1854, Dr. SMITH INGLEHART. (See Family 109.)

---

118. CYNTHIA ELIZA JOHNSON, dau. of Erastus Johnson and Jerusha W. Holt, (115), was born in Cherry Valley, N. Y., July 1, 1824, and died there, July 12, 1887, aged 63.

She married, June 21, 1849, JOHN JUDD,† son of Oliver Judd and Elizabeth Belden. He was born in Cherry Valley, Jan. 28, 1820, his parents coming from New Britain, Conn., in 1804. He was educated in the common school and academy, and at the age of sixteen entered the foundry of his father and was virtually a partner before he was twenty-one. The firm did a flourishing business for many years and several ingenious and useful inventions were

---

* J. B. Dunlap married, 2nd, May 10, 1843, Laura Williams Orcutt, dau. of John Orcutt and Caroline Harrison Williams. She was born in Randolph, Vt., Sept. 11, 1823.

CHILDREN.

1. *Caroline Orcutt,*   b. Apr. 4, 1844.
2. *Hannah Elizabeth,*   b. July 21, 1846; d. Mar. 1, 1847.
3. *Robert Williams,*   b. Jan. 4, 1848;   m. Sept. 12, 1878, Eva Frances Palmer.
4. *Laura Hammond,*   b. Oct. 24, 1850; d. Sept. 6, 1851.
5. *Charles Henry,*   b. Sept. 1, 1852; m. July 1, 1880, Kate Ermegarde Finch.
6. *Mary Irene,*   b. Apr. 12, 1855.

† John Judd married, 1st, Jan. 28, 1845, Martha L. Carey, dau. of Darius H. Carey and Patty Whitney. She was born in Richfield, N. Y., in 1823, and died in Cherry Valley, May 17, 1846, aged 23, leaving no children.

patented and manufactured by them, but very little is done there now. He lives with his eldest children in his native place.

CHILDREN.

1. *Edwin*,   b. Apr. 8, 1850.
2. *Sarah Johnson*, b. Apr. 30, 1852.
3. *Hubert*   b. Aug. 30, 1853; m. Mary A Clark.   (119)
4. *Mary Elizabeth*, b. May 29, 1858; m. Dr. Howard A. Pardee.   (120)

---

119. HUBERT JUDD, son of John Judd and Cynthia E. Johnson, (118), was born in Cherry Valley, N. Y., Aug. 30, 1853. In 1879 he was with a surveying corps in the west, and the following year went to Wallingford, Conn., as an employe of the Judd Manufacturing Company. In 1886 he went to New York City and was with H. L. Judd & Co., nine and one-half years. Dec. 16, 1896, he entered the employ of the Western Electric Co., as receiving clerk. He lives in Brooklyn, N. Y.

He married, Sept. 2, 1885, MARY ADELAIDE CLARK, dau. of Elias Clark and Adelaide Smith. She was born in Rochester, Minn., June 18, 1858.

---

120. MARY ELIZABETH JUDD, dau. of John Judd and Cynthia E. Johnson, (118), was born in Cherry Valley, N. Y., May 29, 1858.

She married, May 17, 1889, Dr. HOWARD ASHLEY PARDEE, son of Augustus Pardee and Emily Kate McKnight. He was born in New York City, Feb. 3, 1859. He graduated from the university of the City of New York in 1880, served as interne in Belevue Hospital 1881–83, then went to Philadelphia, Penn., and is in active practice in that city.

CHILDREN.

1. *Katherine*,   b. Apr. 7, 1890.
2. *Emily McKnight*, b. June 2, 1891.
3. *Howard Judd*,   b. June 13, 1895.

CHERRY VALLEY, N. Y.

Facts concerning the settlement and history, compiled from various sources.

All this part of the state was originally included in Albany county which was organized in 1683 and included the whole colony north and west of its present limits. In 1772 Tryon county (named in honor of Sir William Tryon, then provincial governor of New York) was set off from Albany, and the county seat was located at Johnstown. April 2nd, 1784, its name was changed to Montgomery. On the 16th of February, 1791, Otsego was set off from Montgomery and organized as a separate county.

In 1683 a patent of 8,000 acres lying ten miles south of the Mohawk, and fifty-two west of Albany, was granted by George Clark, Lieut. Governor of the Province of New York, to John Lindesey, Jacob Roseboom, Lendert Gansevoort and Sybrant Van Schaick. Mr. Lindesey having obtained an assignment from the three other patentees to himself and Gov. Clark in 1739, chose for himself a farm and gave it the name of Lindesey's Bush, now the residence of Mr. Edward Phelon. The following summer he brought his family to the place, and having made the acquaintance of the Rev. Samuel Dunlop in New York, prevailed upon him to visit his patent, offering him several hundred acres on condition that he would settle upon it and persuade his friends to accompany him. Thus commenced the settlement of Cherry Valley, but the growth at first was very slow, the number of families in 1775 probably not exceeding sixty. Mr. Dunlop was an Irishman by birth, educated in Edinburgh. He visited Londonderry, in New Hampshire, where some of his countrymen were settled, whom he persuaded to remove, and five or six families came — about thirty persons.

One of the first movements of this little colony was the erection of a rude edifice of logs in which they assembled to worship. Mr. Dunlop opened a classical school in his own house, and students came from the Mohawk valley to avail themselves of his teaching. For some years the Indians were friendly, but from the breaking out of the French and Indian war, 1753-4, until the close of the Revolution there was disturbance and danger. Under British instigation the Indians joined with the Tories, and led by Walter Butler, Tory, and Joseph Brant, Indian, an attack was made on the 11th of Nov., 1778, and a dreadful massacre took place. A fort had been erected the previous summer by the direction of Gen. La Fayette, but through the unwise policy of the commandant there was not time for the inhabitants to reach the fort. Some few made their escape but thirty-two were killed, together with fourteen Continental soldiers, the houses were burnt, and between thirty and forty prisoners were taken to Canada. The following spring the fort was abandoned, the troops joining Sullivan's expedition at Otsego Lake. At the close of the war the remnant of the inhabitants returned to their former homes and a few log houses were built. A touching record is preserved of the meeting in the burial ground for the rehabilitation of the church.

In October, 1783, Gen. Washington, accompanied by Gen. George Clinton and others, visited the place and were guests of Col. Samuel Campbell, on their way to Otsego Lake and the head waters of the Susquehanna. The return of life to the little colony was a hard struggle for some years. The early history of this frontier was published in 1831 in "The Annals of Tryon County," by William W. Campbell. In that work it is narrated that " Rev. Solomon Spaulding, the reputed author of the Mormon Bible, or rather of a novel in which he undertook to show that the American Indians were the descendants of the ten Lost Tribes of Israel (the manuscript of which afterwards came into the possession of the famous Joseph Smith, and constituted the Golden Leaves), had been preaching for a time and teaching in the new academy." The school was opened in July, 1796, but on the 24th of the following Oct., at a meeting of the trustees it was " Voted that Mr. Spaulding be dismissed from any further attendance on the School in the academy and that the Senior Trustee inform of this Resolution. Adjourned."

In 1795 the Rev. Eliphalet Nott visited Cherry Valley, and the following year returned with his wife, as preacher in the church and teacher in the academy. The latter, described as a spacious building 60x40 feet, had been erected and a charter granted in February, 1796. Mr. Nott remained two years; after he left, the church was not regularly supplied for some years, but the academy seems to have been continued with almost no interruptions, acquiring wide celebrity as a young ladies' seminary from 1851 to 1862. During the war of the Rebellion the institution became financially embarrassed but struggled on till 1866. In the vacation of that year, on the 5th of July, a disastrous fire swept away an old established hotel; a still more important hotel had been burnt four weeks earlier, and the emergency led to what was expected to be only a temporary occupation of the academy property for hotel purposes. The school, so interrupted, could not be revived; the property became alienated, and thus the grand old Academy, the mother of so many cultivated men and women, passed out of existence. In the years 1851-2 two wings of three stories each had been erected for the accomodation of boarding pupils; the building, well adapted for hotel purposes, had quite recently been extensively remodeled as a summer resort, water being brought in pipes from a mineral spring to add to the attractions of the place. On the 6th of July, 1894, the structure was leveled to the ground by fire, the fourth hotel in the village destroyed in less than thirty years, all of them supposed to be by the torch of the incendiary. An academic school was again opened in 1881; in 1890 a board of trustees was formed and the school was received by the Regents of the University under the old charter as the Cherry Valley Academy. In 1895 it was replaced by an academic department in the district, a Union Free school.

The following is a copy of the old Charter: "The Regents of the University of the State of New York: To all to whom these Presents shall come, Greeting:

Whereas, Eli Parsons, Ephraim Hudson and thirty-nine other persons by an instrument in writing under their hands and seals dated the first day of January last, after stating among other things that they have at great expense and trouble erected a spacious House in the Town of Cherry Valley for the express purpose of a Seminary of Learning, and that one acre of Land and Eight Hundred Pounds have been given for the benefit of the same, did make application to us, the said Regents, that the said Seminary of Learning or Academy might be incorporated by the name of the Trustees of the Cherry Valley Academy and become subject to our visitation, and that the persons hereinafter mentioned might be the first Trustees thereof. Now Know Ye, that We, the said Regents having enquired into the allegations contained in the instrument in writing aforesaid, and finding the same to be true and conceiving the said Academy calculated for the promotion of Literature, Do by these presents pursuant to the Statute in such case made and provided, signify our approbation of the Incorporation of Eli Parsons, Luther Rich, Benjamin Rathbone, Lester Holt, Samuel Campbell, Ephraim Hudson, Ozias Waldo, Christopher P. Yates, William White, Junior, Robert Dickson, Thomas Whitacar, Simeon Rich, Joseph White, Elijah Holt and Richard Edwards, the Trustees of the said Academy named by the said Founders thereof, in the instrument in writing above mentioned by the name of Trustees of the Cherry Valley Academy.

In Witness thereof we have caused our Common Seal to be hereunto affixed the eighth day of February, in the twentieth year of the Independence of the United States of America Annoque Domini one thousand seven hundred and ninety six.

     Witness John Jay Esquire, Chancellor of the University
     John Jay, (L. S.) De Witt Clinton, Sec'y.

On the fourth of July, 1840, was celebrated the centennial of the settlement of Cherry Valley, on which occasion many of its friends gathered and listened to a historical address by the Hon. W. W. Campbell. In 1868 a monument was erected in a conspicuous place in the centre of the village, to the memory of those who fell in the war of the rebellion. The Centennial fourth of July, 1876, duly celebrated, was marked by the publication of a "Historical Account of the Presbyterian Church," by the pastor, first delivered in a series of sermons. The project often made of erecting a monument to commemorate the massacre of 1778 was followed up and money raised. In the centennial year, 1878, the work was completed, the 15th of August was fixed upon for the unveiling, and many of Cherry Valley's sons and daughters returned to do honor to the occasion. The principal address was by Major Douglas Campbell, a great-grandson of Col. Samuel Campbell; other speakers were Hon. Horatio Seymour, Hon. S. C. Willson, of Indiana, Hon. W. W. Snow, of Oneonta.

One of the early residents in Cherry Valley was Dr. Joseph White, who after the completion of his medical course came here to settle in 1787. He became a very eminent surgeon, his practice extending from Albany to Buffalo. In 1800 he was appointed first judge of the court of common pleas for Otsego County, and held that office till 1822. In 1817 he was chosen president of the medical college at Fairfield, Herkimer County, N. Y., and the following year was chosen the first president of the Cherry Valley bank. He died June 2, 1832.

The Hon. Levi Beardsley was another of the early residents, who came from Richfield in 1810 to study law with Jabez D. Hammond, and rose to eminence in his profession. He was a member of the state legislature two terms, 1830 to 1837, and the last year of his second term was president of the senate. In 1839 he left Cherry Valley for Oswego, and subsequently opened a law office in New York in 1846. In 1852 he published a volume of " Reminiscences; Personal and other incidents; Early settlement of Otsego County; Notices and anecdotes of public men; Judicial, legal and legistative matters; Field sports; Dissertations and discussions." A book full of interest.

APPENDIX.

a. Johannes Roseboom married, Nov. 18, 1688, Gerritje Coster, dau. of Hendrick Coster and Geertje Goosense Van Schaick. He was buried Jan. 25, 1745.

CHILDREN.

1. *Hendrick,* bap. Aug. 4, 1689.
2. *Johannes,* " Apr. 23, 1692.
3. *Johannes,* " Apr. 29, 1694.
4. *Gerrit,* " Feb. 17, 1697.
5. *Elizabeth,* " Apr. 28, 1700.
6. *Geertruy,* " Dec. 27, 1702.
7. *Margarita,* " Apr. 21, 1706.
8. *Anna,* " Apr. 21, 1706; m. Mar. 20, 1735, Sybrant Van Schaick.

b. Margarita Roseboom married, Nov. 15, 1685, Pieter Thomase Mingael, son of Thomas Janse Mingael and Maritje Abrahamse Vosburgh. He died in 1706. There is no record of any children.

c. * Gerrit Roseboom was born July 12, 1663, and died Dec. 27, 1739, aged 76. He was married, in Albany, by Dominie Delius, Nov. 4, 1689, to Maria Sanders, dau. of Robert T. Sanders and Elsie Barentse. She was born Aug. 28, 1666, and was buried July 10, 1741, aged 74.

CHILDREN.

1. *Hendrick,* b. Dec. 15, 1690; m. Debora
2. *Robert,* " May 20, 1693; m. Oct. 17, 1743, Rykje Roseboom; d. Feb. 12, 1764, [ae. 70.
3. *Elsje,* " Sep. 15, 1695.
4. *Gysbert,* " Dec. 12, 1697; m. Dec. 4, 1720, Catharine Bries; d. Oct. 29, 1749, [ae. 51.
5. *Ahasuerus,* " Jan. 12, 1699; m. Nov. 25, 1725, Maritie Bratt; she was bur. Nov. [30, 1745.
6. *Johannes,* " Mar. 29, 1702.
7. *Elizabeth,* " July 21, 1704; d. Mar. 10, 1727, ae. 22.

* This record has been translated from the original entries in Dutch, in the Bible of Gerrit Roseboom, now in the possession of Mrs. Ford Williams, of Chatham Center, Columbia Co., N. Y.

132   APPENDIX.

d. Hendrick Roseboom married, Nov. 1, 1694, Debora Staats, dau. of Jacob (?) Staats. She was buried Oct. 2, 1749.

CHILDREN.

1. *Jacob*,   bap.   July 14, 1695; m. Aug. 12, 1716, Geertruy Lydius; she was bur. [July 27, 1757.
2. *Elizabeth*,   "   June 6, 1697.
3. *Rykje*,   "   Oct. 13, 1700; m. Oct. 17, 1743, Robert Roseboom.
4. *Hendrick*,   "   Mar. 3, 1703;   m. Oct. 25, 1724, Elsie Cuyler; he was bur. Oct. 29, [1754, ae. 51.
5. *Catherine*,   "   June 16, 1706.
6. *Margarieta*,   "   Oct. 19, 1712.
7. *Abraham*,   "   Jan. 9, 1715.

---

e. Elizabeth Roseboom married, Jan. 13, 1692, Willem Jacobse Van Deusen, son of Jacob Abrahamse Van Deusen and Catalyntie Van Eslant. He was buried Sept. 8, 1731.

CHILDREN.

1. *Jacob*,   bap.   Sept. 4, 1692.
2. *Margariet*,   "   Apr. 14, 1695.
3. *Catalyntje*,   "   Nov. 21, 1697; m. July 15, 1721, Jan Oothout; she d. May 13, 1753, [ae. 55; he d. Aug. 20, 1739.
4. *Marytje*,   "   Sept. 1, 1700.
5. *Elizabeth*,   "   Mar. 21, 1703.
6. *Henrik*,   "   Dec. 25, 1705; m.   Ariaantje Staats.
7. *Elizabeth*,   "   Dec. 25, 1705.

---

f. Record of Dutch Church Baptisms, Annals of Albany, Vol. III.

CHILDREN OF JOHANNES ROSEBOOM AND GERRITJE COSTER.

Children.   *Sponsors.*

1. *Hendrick*,   1689, Hendrick Roseboom.
2. *Johannes*,   1692, Gerrit Roseboom, Gysbertje Roseboom.
3. *Johannes*,   1694.
4. *Gerrit*,   1697.
5. *Elizabeth*,   1700, Elizabeth Roseboom.
6. *Geertruy*,   1702, Hendrick Roseboom, Sr.
7. *Margarita*,   1706, Myndert Roseboom, Debora Roseboom.
8. *Anna*,

CHILDREN OF GERRIT ROSEBOOM AND MARIA SANDERS.

1. *Robert*,   1693, Robert Sanders.
2. *Elsje*,   1695, Johannes Roseboom.
3. *Gysbert*,   1697.
4. *Ahasuerus*,   1700.
5. *Johannes*,   1702.
6. *Elizabeth*,   1704.

Children of Hendrick Roseboom and Debora Staats.

1. *Jacob,* 1695.
2. *Elizabeth,* 1697, Hendrick Roseboom, Sr.
3. *Rykje,* 1700, Johannes Roseboom.
4. *Hendrick,* 1703, Gerrit Roseboom, Gerritje Roseboom.
5. *Margarita,* 1706, Myndert Roseboom.
6. *Catharina,* Oct. 12, 1712.
7. *Abraham,* Jan. 9, 1715.

Children of Willem Jacobse Van Deusen and Elizabeth Roseboom.

1. *Jacob,* 1692, Herbert Jacobs, Gysbertje Roseboom.
2. *Margriet,* 1695, Hendrick Roseboom, Catalina Jacobs.
3. *Catelyntie,* 1697, Johannes Roseboom.
4. *Maryte,* 1700, Gerritje Roseboom.
5. *Elizabeth,* 1703, Gerrit Roseboom, Maryte Van Duse.
6. *Hendrick,*
7. *Elizabeth,* 1705, Hendrick Roseboom, Debora Roseboom, Maryte Van Duse.

---

g. Dutch Church Burials. Annals of Albany. Vol. 1.

1722. Oct. 1, Jacob Roseboom's child.
1722. Oct. 22, Myndert Roseboom.
1722. Dec. 18, Maria Roseboom's daughter.
1723. Sep. 17, Jacob Roseboom's child.
1726. Sep. 11, Jacob Roseboom's child.
1727, Mar. 12, Gerrit Roseboom's daughter.
1732, Jan. 6, Hendrick Roseboom's child.
1732, May 20, Hendrick H. Roseboom's child.
1733, Feb. 16, Sarah Roseboom was buried, daughter of Jacob Roseboom.
1734, Aug. 12, Gysbert Roseboom's child.
1735; Nov. 3, Hendrick H. Roseboom's child.
1738, Sep. 17, Hendrick M. Roseboom's child.
1738, Oct. 17, Hendrick H. Roseboom's child.
1739, Dec. 21, Gerrit Roseboom.
1741, Apr. 9, Margarietie, daughter of Maria Roseboom.
1741, July 10, Maria Roseboom.
1745, Jan. 25, John Roseboom — Buried under the church.
1745, Nov. 30, Asueros Roseboom's wife.
1746, July 20, Debora, dau. of Hendrick H. Roseboom.
1746, Aug. 15, Hendrick H. Roseboom.
1746, Nov. 23, Gerritie Roseboom, in the church.
1748, Jan. 14, Little son of Catalyntie Roseboom.
1749, Oct. 2, Debora Roseboom.
1749, Oct. 29, Gysbert Roseboom.
1751, Oct. 30, Wife of John G. Roseboom.
1753, Nov. 7, John Roseboom (Doxter).
1754, Oct. 29, Hendrick Roseboom.
1757, July 27, Wife of Jacob Roseboom.

134   APPENDIX.

h. Know All Men By These Presents. That upon the 16th day of July 1686, in Albany Mr. Robt. Sanders, inhabitant at this city did purchase for his daughter Mary aged about 18 years a certain tract or parcell of land lying on ye Long Reach on ye east side oft Hudson's River on ye Wappinges Creek, reaching up ye creek on a place called Keechkachkameeck. And again westerly on ye river side to a place called Agawarelinck, in which bounds is comprehended three valleys or marshes and all creeks and kells that lie within ye same, and that of certain highland Indians called Nassiehampeet, who is also called Souwen-wes, and his wife Wauwelinneek, who is also called Ann, his Brother Quackwoof Jochquamin, another Indian squa called Nakenewon, and ye son of Ann called Rochquamock, for which parcell of land they acknowledged to have received full satisfaction of Robt. Sanders afforesaid. Therefore ye said Indian proprietors do transport ye said parcell of land, as they do by these presents to ye afforesaid Mary daughter of Robt. Sanders in full possession and propriety, for her and her heirs and assigns, or to them that hereafter may title and action, really and actually by these presents. And ye said Indian owners do desist and quit claim to all there action and protension that they had to ye above land for now and ever hereafter.

Which said piece of land is comprehended in a certain grant which ye said Mary hath obtained of ye Right Honble. Col. Thomas Dongan Gov. Genl., Dated ye 28, day of May 1686.

Was Signed and Sealed by

	Nassi Hampeet	L. S.
Indian Witnesses	Wanwe Linnick	L. S.
Tataomsiant	Quaehwoot	L. S
Massany	Jochquamin	L. S.
	Nalenow	L. S.
	Rookquamok	L. S.

In presence of me John Baker, Notary Public.

This was signed and sealed in the presence of us

Jan Jansse Bleeker,   Justice of ye Peace.
J. Lend Cuyler   Justice of ye Peace.

List oy ye payments that ye Indians and ye wives have Recd. for ye purchase of ye land for which they declared to have full satisfaction in full. Two Gunns — Four Great Kittolls — Six Faddon Dusstolls — A White Blanket — Four Fatts of Rum — Hondert Awls — Hondert Needles — 1 Half Fatt Good Beer — 12 Knives — 1 Roll Tobacco — 2 Shirts — 1 Brave Christian Coat — 2 Axes — Another Small Gunn.

Translated out of ye original P. me Robt. Livingston.

---

i. By the Honourable Cadwallander Colden, Esq., President of His Majesty's Council, and Commander in Chief of the Province of New York, and the Territories depending thereon in America. To Myndert Roseboom Esquire Greeting. Reposing especial Trust and Confidence, as well in the

Care, Diligence, and Circumspection, as in the Loyalty, Courage and Readiness of You, to do His Majesty good and faithful Service: have nominated, constituted and appointed, and I DO, by Virtue of the Powers and Authorities to Me given by His Majesty, hereby nominate, constitute and appoint You the said Myndert Roseboom to be Lieutenant Colonel of the Second Regiment of the Forces in the Pay of the Province of New York whereof George Brewerton Esq'r is Colonel. You are therefore to take the said Regiment into your Charge and Care, as Lieutenant Colonel thereof, and duly to exercise both the Officers and Soldiers of that Regiment in Arms. And as they are hereby commanded to obey You as their Lieutenant Colonel, so are you likewise to observe and follow such Orders and Directions, from time to time, as you shall receive from Me, or any other your Superior Officer, according to the Rules and Dicipline of War, in Pursuance of the Trust reposed in you: and for so doing, this shall be your Commission.

Given under my Hand and Seal at Arms, in New York, the sixth day of April in the first Year of His Majesty's Reign, Annoque Domini One Thousand Seven Hundred and Sixty One. Cadwallander Colden.

By his Honour's Command.
G Banyer, Sec'y.

---

j. This Indenture made the First day of February in the Year of our Lord one thousand seven hundred and seventy-five, Between John Harper of the County of Tryon, Husbandman, of the one part And Myndert Roseboom* of the City of Albany, Merchant, of the other part Witnesseth that he the said John Harper for and in Consideration of the sum of Three hundred and Eighty six pounds Current money of New York to him the said John Harper by him the said Myndert Roseboom in hand paid at and before the En-sealing and Delivery of these presents the Receipt Whereof he the said John Harper doth hereby Acknowledge and thereof and of every Part and parcell thereof doth acquit. Release and Discharge him the said Myndert Roseboom his heirs and assigns for ever by these presents he the said John Harper hath granted Bargained sold Aliened Remised Released and confirmed and by these presents doth grant Bargain, Sell, Alien, Remise Release and confirm unto him the said Myndert Roseboom his heirs and assigns for ever (being now in his Actual Possession) all that Lott of Land Called or known by the Name of Lott Number Two, being part of a Tract of Land of five hundred acres formerly patented to John Lindesay in the County of Albany, Which Said Tract was afterwards Devided into two Lotts and distinguished by the Names of Lott Number One and Lott Number Two as by the Draft and Devision thereof made by Edward Collins Deputy Surveyor may more fully appear.

---

* After the first part of this book was printed, a record was found at Albany, (356, 2137) Aug. 14th, 1770, of a "Royal," (not military) grant of 45,000 acres of land in Albany county, to forty-five persons named, of whom Myndert Roseboom was one. The tract extended from a creek named Hay-ad-er-es-se-ras to Sackindaga, or West branch of the Hudson, and lay chiefly in Edinburgh and Providence, Saratoga county.

Together with all and Singular the woods underwoods Trees, Timbers, feeding Pastures, Meadows, Marshes, Swamps, ways, waters, water courses, Rivers, Brooks, Rivulets, Runs and Streams of water, Fishing, fowling, hunting and hawking, Mines, Minerals of all sorts whatsoever,—Except Gold mines and Silver mines,—which now or hereafter Shall be Standing growing, lying, being or to be found in or upon the aforesaid Lott Number Two or any part or parcell thereof, and the Reversion and Reversions Remainder and Remainders, Rents, Issues and profitts thereof and of every part and parcell thereof and also all the Estate Right Title Interest property possession Claim and Demand Whatsoever of him the said John Harper of in or to the name or any part or parcell thereof to have and to hold the said Lott Number Two and all other the hereby granted premises aforesaid and every part and parcell thereof with their and every of their Appurtenences unto him the said Myndert Roseboom his heirs and Assigns for Ever Subject to the payment of the Quit Rents due and hereafter to be due unto his Majesty, his heirs and Successors from the Twenty fifth day of March one thousand seven hundred and forty three and also Subject to and under the Several Exceptions, Reservations, Restrictions and Limitations in and by his Majesty's Letters Patent for the said Tract of land mentioned and expressed And he the said John Harper and his heirs all and Singular the before Granted premises with the Appurtenences and every part and parcell thereof unto him the said Myndert Roseboom his heirs and Assigns and Against all and every other person and persons Whatsoever Lawfully Claiming or to claim any Estate Right Title or Interest of in or to the said hereby granted premises or any part or parcell thereof by From or Under him them any or either of them shall and will warrant and forever Defend by these Presents. In Witness thereof The parties to these presents have hereunto Interchangeably set their hands and Seals the day and Year first above written.

(Sig.) John Harper (L. S.)

Sealed and delivered in the presence of Sam'l Pruyn, John Fred. Pruyn.

Memorandum that on the first day of February one thousand seven hundred & seventy five personally appeared before me, Jacob C. Ten Eyck Judge of the Inferior Court of the City and County of Albany the within named John Harper of Harpersfield in the County of Tryon Acknowledge the within Deed or Instrument to be his Voluntary Act & Deed for the Purpose therein mentioned and I have Examined the within Instrument & find no material Reazurds (erasures) or Interlindations therein I therefore allow the Same to be Recorded.   Jacob C. Ten Eyck.

I do hereby Acknowledge to have received from Myndert Roseboom the Sum of Three hundred Eighty-six pounds New York Currency in full for the within Consideration money in Witness I hereby sett my hand. Albany February the first, one thousand seven hundred Seventy-five.

(Sig.) John Harper.

---

k. This Indenture made the twelfth day of March, in the year of our Lord one thousand seven hundred and ninety-five, between George Clarke of

Hyde, in the county of Chester and Kingdom of Great Britian, by William Banyer of the City of Albany, in the County of Albany, his Attorney, of the first part, and John Roseboom of the Town of Canajoharie, in the County of Montgomery and State of New York, of the second part, Witnesseth, that the said party of the first part for and in consideration of the sum of five hundred pounds, of lawful money of the State of New York, to him in hand paid at or before the sealing and delivery of these presents, the receipt whereof is hereby acknowledged, hath granted, bargained, sold, aliened, released and confirmed and by these presents doth grant, bargain, sell, alien, release and confirm unto the said party of the second part, and to his heirs and assigns forever,

All that certain tract or parcel of land situate, lying and being in the County of Otsego, in a Patent granted on the twenty-fourth day of May, one thousand seven hundred and thirty-nine unto John Lindsley, and which said tract or parcel of land is known and distinguished by the name of lot No. one and begins at a marked white Ash tree and runs thence south five degrees forty minutes west, fifty-two chains and fifty links; thence south twenty-nine degrees thirty minutes west, six-two chains and fifty links; thence West eleven chains and fifty links; thence north thirteen degrees east one hundred and twenty-three chains and fifty links; thence south fifty-two degrees east, twenty-four chains and forty links to the place where it first began, containing two hundred and fifty acres of land.

Together with all and singular the appurtenances, privileges and advantages whatsoever unto the above mentioned and described premises in anywise appertaining or belonging, and the reversion and reversions, remainder and remainders, rents, issues and profits thereof, and also all the estate, right, title, interest, property, claim and demand whatsoever as well in law as in equity, of the said party of the first part, of in and to the same or any part or parcel thereof with the appurtenances. To have and to hold the above granted, bargained and decribed premises and every part and parcel thereof, with the appurtenances, unto the said party of the second part, his heirs and assigns to the only proper use and behoof of the said party of the second part, his heirs and assigns forever, and to and for no other use, intent or purpose whatsoever and the said party of the first part for himself, his heirs, executors and administrators, doth covenent, grant, promise and agree to and with the said party of the second part, his heirs and assigns, that he the said party of the first part at the time of the sealing and delivery of these presents is lawfully and rightfully seized in his own right of a good, sure, perfect, absolute and indefeasible estate of inheritance in fee simple of and in all and singular and said premises above mentioned, with the appurtenances without any manner of condition to alter, change, determine or defeat the same, and hath in himself good right, full power and lawful authority to grant, bargain, sell, convey and release the above said described land and premises with the appurtenances, unto the said party of the second part his heirs and assigns in manner and form aforesaid. And also that he the said party of the first part and his heirs the said tract or parcel of land, and all and singular other the premises herein before mentioned or intended to be hereby granted, bargained, sold, released and confirmed and every part and parcel thereof with the appurtenances unto the said party of the second part his heirs and assigns against him the said party of the first part and his heirs and against all other persons whomsoever, any estate having or lawfully claiming of, in, to or out of the said premises, or of, in and to any part or parcel thereof with the appurtenances, or that shall or may claim by, from or under or in trust for him or them or any of them, shall and will Warrant and forever Defend by these presents.

In Witness Whereof the parties to these presents have hereunto set their hands and seals the day and year first above written.

  Sealed and delivered in the presence of us.

               Geo. Clarke, by his Atty.
                Willm. Banyer.

The word "two" in ninth line written on an erasure and the words "and fifty" above same line interlined.

               Geo. Banyer Jr.
               Ab. Van Vechten.

Be it remembered that on the twelfth day of August in the year of Our Lord, one thousand seven hundred and ninety-seven, personally appeared before me, John Lansing Jun. one of the Justices of the Supreme Court of Judicature of the State of New York, the within named Geo. Clarke, who acknowledged that the within named William Banyer as his Atty., had executed the within written Indenture and that the same was the deed of him, the said Geo. Clarke and having examined the said Indenture and finding therein no erasure, interlineation or obliteration (other than those noted) and being personally acquainted with the said George and satisfied he is the person described as Grantor in the said Indenture, I allow the same to be recorded.

               John Lansing Jun.

Recorded Oct. 22, 1801, at 8 o'clock P.M., in Book D of Conveyances page 124.

---

1. In the Name of God Amen. I Hendrick M. Roseboom of the City and County of Albany being weak in body, but of sound Memory and Understanding praised be God for the same, and considering this transitory life, Do make publish and declare this my last Will and Testament in manner and form following. that is to say First and principally I recommend my Soul into the hands of God my Creator hoping a pardon for all my Sins thro the Merits of Jesus Christ my blessed Redeemer, my body I commit to the Earth to be decently interred, at the discretion of my Executor herein after Named, as to such worldly Estate wherewith God hath been pleased to bless me, I dispose of the same as follows: Imprimis I will order and direct that all my just debts and funeral Expenses be paid and satisfied by my said Executor. Item I give devise and bequeath unto my Son Johannes Roseboom and to his heirs and assigns forever, All my Estate both Real and personal, which I at present am possessed of, or which I hold in Reversion or Remainder, Subject-

ing Nevertheless my said Son Johannes his heirs and assigns after my decease to pay or cause to be paid unto my Sons Myndert Roseboom and Barent Roseboom for and during their Natural Lives each a yearly sum of money equal to one third of the Rent receiveable for my House and Lot of Ground situate in Maiden Lane in the second Ward of the City of Albany. Lastly I do hereby Nominate and Appoint my said Son Johannes Roseboom the sole Executor of this my last Will and Testament, and I do hereby Revoke and make void all former Wills and Testaments by me at any time heretofore Made, In Witness whereof I have hereunto set my hand and seal this twenty-seventh day of July — in the Year of our Lord one thousand seven hundred and ninety

Hendrick Roseboom.

Witnesses: P. W. Douw, Henry Ten Eyck, Nicholas Fonda.

III. In the Name of God Amen, I Barent Roseboom, Batchelor formerly of the City of Albany but at present Residing at Canajoharie in Montgomery County in the State of New York being weak of body but of sound and disposing mind and Memory (praised be God) Do make ordain publish and declare this my last Will and Testament in Manner following.

I Will that all my just debts and funeral Charges be paid. I give and Bequeath unto my loving Brother Myndert Roseboom the Sum of Twenty Pounds. I give and Bequeath unto my Brother John Roseboom the Sum of Five Pounds. I give and Bequeath unto Elizabeth Roseboom eldest daughter of John Roseboom and Wife of Conrad Gansevoort my Negro Wench Dion and an Iron plate Chimney Back. I give and Bequeath unto my Brothers Son Barent Roseboom all the Land belonging to me in Whiteburgh and the one Half of what I am to Heir from John Myndert Roseboom and likewise the one Fifth Part of All my other Property both Real and Personal not herein Willed I give and Bequeath unto my Brother's Son John Roseboom my Right to a Lot Ground in Albany on the Hill at present in possession of Samuel Bromley and One Fifth share of all my other Property. I give and Bequeath unto my Brother's Son Abraham Roseboom One Hundred Pounds and Interest due thereon Six Weeks after my decease and One-Fifth Part of my other Property. I give & Bequeath unto my Brother's youngest daughter Maria Roseboom Fifty Pounds and a Fifth Part of my other Property. I further Will that my Brothers daughter Elizabeth Roseboom likewise have a fifth share of all my property not before Willed. I give and Bequeath unto the daughter of Johannes Ten Eyck named Neilte Ten Eyck my Psalm Book. I give and Bequeath unto Barent Schermerhorn Son of Jacob Schermerhorn of Green Bush a Silver Spoon marked Janitie Ten Eyck tyed with a Black crape round it. I will that whatever is due to me from Arent Van Duersen be freely forgiven him. And Lastly I constitute and make my Loving Brother John Roseboom and his Son Barent Roseboom and Conrad Gansevoort Executors of this my Last Will & Testament and I do hereby utterly Disallow Revoke and Disannul all former and other Wills

Legacies and Executors by me heretofore made Willed and Bequeathed Ratyfying and confirming this and no other to be my last Will & Testament. In Witness whereof I have hereunto set my Hand and Seal this Twenty-fourth day of December in the year of our Lord One thousand Seven Hundred and Ninty-five.

BAR'T ROSEBOOM.

Witnesses: Daniel Hegerman, John J. Roseboom, John Diell.

www.ingramcontent.com/pod-product-compliance
Lightning Source LLC
Chambersburg PA
CBHW030338170426
43202CB00010B/1163